WHAT OTHERS ARE SAYING ABOUT THIS AMAZING BOOK:

One of the major crimes of our day is identity theft. In contemporary society the crime impacts what we own but the Father of Lies has been engaged in identity theft since the beginning of time and it impacts who we are and destiny. We are called to grow up into maturity in all ways like Jesus Christ. When we attempt to be and do what Jesus has called us to be the lie comes like a questions: "Who do you think you are?" Paul countered the lie in his letter to the church in Corinth with the voice of truth and Bob Burney challenges us to remember who we are and whose we are in Christ. We are to be living on the resurrection side of the cross where we are free to live and to be all that Jesus Christ has called us to be. Get ready to be transformed as you: **Remember Whose You Are!**

-David Ruleman
Vice President of Operations
Salem Communications Washington DC

⸺⸺❧•❧⸺⸺

It has been my pleasure to know Bob Burney for over 30 years. Whether in the pulpit, on the mission field, or across radio airwaves, Bob is always on the cutting edge of faithfully communicating God's Word to believers and non-believers alike in an inspiring and challenging way. And his new book is no different.
You will be greatly blessed as you see God's care for you unfold in such a personal and dynamic way!

-Frank Carl
Pastor of Genoa Baptist Church, Westerville, Ohio

⸺⸺❧•❧⸺⸺

Just look around and you will discover that many Christians are facing an identity crisis. Although the Bible warns us not to be "conformed to this world" it seems that a large portion of the Evangelical community has forgotten not only who they are, but also whose they are. Bob Burney deals with this problem head-on in his new book. In **REMEMBER WHOSE YOU ARE!**, *he reminds Christians of their unspeakable spiritual wealth in Christ while also reminding them that they have been purchased with the precious* *blood of Jesus. This book unveils the powerful strategy that the Apostle Paul used to bring about an incredible revival in the carnal church at Corinth. The same kind of personal and corporate revival is still possible today if we could understand this powerful principle. You will never be the same once you understand, "Whose you are."*

-Dr. Robert Jeffress
Senior Pastor
First Baptist Church
Dallas, TX

We've got an identity problem in America—especially in the Evangelical community. I have found throughout my ministry that few people really understand who are they, spiritually. Paul clearly tells us in Ephesians that God has already given us all spiritual blessing in Christ Jesus. That makes us spiritual millionaires! Yet, most are living like they are spiritual paupers. God doesn't want us to live in a spiritual ghetto. Bob Burney addresses this problem in his new book **Remember Whose You Are***! His biblically balanced approach to our position in Christ is a must read for any Christian struggling with determining who they are by reminding them of whose they are. I believe that anyone who reads this book will be encouraged in a powerful way to see their relationship with Christ in a new way.*

-Fred Luter
Pastor of Franklin Avenue Baptist Church in New Orleans
President of the Southern Baptist Convention

Bob Burney writes clearly, offers solid biblical truth, and provides practical questions to help you apply the content to your life. You will find in these pages a great resource that discusses the opening of 1 Corinthians and several biblical characters. If you want to grow closer to God and be challenged in your faith, then I recommend you read this book and take the "reflect and apply" questions seriously.
-Thomas White
President, Cedarville University

Bob Burney is more than a terrific communicator, he's a master chef. In one easy-to-read volume, Bob has taken one of the meatiest chapters in the Bible and served it up as one of the most delicious too. Whereas every word of scripture is food for the soul, some passages just have more protein than others. The first chapter of I Corinthians is one of those chapters. Bob has unwrapped Paul's words into a birthright meal. From the opening course of WHO We Are, to the dessert of WHOSE We Are, every morsel is well prepared and oh so satisfying.

-Ron Walters
Senior Vice President of Ministry Relations
Salem Communications

By looking at how the Apostle Paul dealt with the terribly dysfunctional church at Corinth, Bob Burney provides a powerful reminder of what it means to be purchased by the blood of Christ.

-Janet Meffered
Host, The Janet Mefferd Show
Nationally syndicated on the Salem Radio Network

Yes, this is a study of 1 Corinthians, but you'll find out quickly that this book is all about YOU! I would venture to say that when a born-again believer hears Bob Burney or someone else say, "Remember Whose You Are!" they immediately think, "I belong to God." What most people don't do is to think about what that really means. They fail to consider what they HAVE NOW as a result of being a child of God. If you've ever worried once or had concerns about your life, you'll find hope, comfort and confidence as you read. If you don't yet have a personal relationship with God through His Son, Jesus Christ, I believe you will see there is much to be gained in beginning that relationship today.

-Dan Craig
Manager of Programming
Moody Radio

REMEMBER
WHOSE YOU ARE!
Discover Your Identity in Christ

Bob Burney

Remember Whose You Are!
Discover Your Identity in Christ
by Bob Burney

Printed in the United States of America

ISBN 9781629522586

www.xulonpress.com

DEDICATION

This book is dedicated first to my Savior Jesus Christ. It is He who bought me and made me His own. I am His and He is mine.

I also dedicate it to my wonderful wife, Joy. She has been my life partner, my best friend, my biggest supporter and true Help Meet for over 44 years. It's in great part her encouragement that caused me to finally write what had been in my heart for years. She truly is the Joy of my life.

TABLE OF CONTENTS

ACKNOWLEDGEMENTS

I am thankful for the people at Xulon Press who have so kindly held my hand and walked me through the publishing process. I am also thankful for the support I have received from Salem Communications. I count it an honor to be associated with our team at WRFD Radio in Columbus, Ohio and the entire corporate family. My general manager, Tom Heyl has been a special encouragement through this process. I am grateful for the proofreading of Pastor Paul Gabriel who graciously agreed to give his valuable input to the manuscript

    I would like to especially acknowledge the assistance of my editor, Dr. Larry Keefauver. This first time author will be eternally grateful for his invaluable assistance, knowledge, skills and expertise.

Introduction

GOD'S WAITING ROOM

For the preaching of the Cross is to them that perish, foolishness. But unto us who are saved, it is the power of God. (1 Corinthians 1:18)

At times, I have wondered how many books have gone unwritten. I'm not sure that's grammatically correct but I think you know what I mean. Bookshelves, coffee tables, libraries, and now Kindles and Nooks around the world contain millions of books by millions of authors. But I imagine that there are probably even more books that reside only in the heart and mind of authors who have a story to tell, an experience to share, and lessons to be learned. Yet for a thousand different reasons or excuses, they have never put those thoughts to print.

I have had several books in my heart for a number of years now. I have no delusions that my thoughts are any more important than those penned by the countless authors who have long before me put their heart and soul on a page, but I do believe God has given me a message to share. Our gracious God has given me a wonderful family, a life time of ministry to the Church, and a long and blessed position of influence through the radio. It has not been an easy road, however. As my wife and I share our hearts through CrossPower Ministries (www.crosspower. net), we try to make it abundantly clear that when we come to minister in a local church we are not coming as "experts" with all the answers. We are coming as two who have been brought to brokenness on many occasions and on many levels, and have been sustained by the power of the finished work of Jesus Christ on the Cross. It is a message we love to proclaim, but it is also a message we are continually learning.

We have found that it is impossible to explore fully the depths of all that Jesus accomplished through His glorious death, burial, and resurrection. We have found that I Corinthians 1:18 is completely true, "For the preaching of the Cross is to them that perish, foolishness. But unto us who are saved, it is the power of God." This book flows out of many years now of trying to both understand and to live that truth. It is my sincere prayer that the promise of the power of God that comes with the proclamation of the cross will in some measure flow to all who read the words contained in this work.

As I said before, this book has been in my heart for many years. You might be interested in what finally pushed me to stop procrastinating and begin the painstaking work of communicating heart to ink and paper. As I write these words, I am recovering from one of the most difficult experiences of my life. I won't bore you with the details, but I am currently recovering from surgery on my neck. I just passed through the worst pain I have ever experienced due to ruptured disks in my neck. I can't express the severity of the pain. While I am certain there are countless people who have experienced far worse pain and probably for a much longer time, for me this was my pinnacle of physical suffering. Surgery would relieve the pain, but was delayed for a considerable time because of medications that had to leave my blood stream. The wait and pain were the perfect storm it seemed. My sweet wife and I counted down the days until the surgery.

After surgery, the pain was almost instantly relieved. The doctor assured us that the recovery would be quick and I would soon be back to preaching and hosting my daily radio program at WRFD Radio in Columbus, Ohio.

Oh yes, there was a small risk that my voice might be affected as the surgery was very close to the vocal chords. However, even if it was affected, it should be for a very short period of time. As I sit here at my computer, I can only whisper and that for just a few words. My return to the radio and preaching has been delayed with no real definitive word on when my voice will return. I have been told that there is a chance that I will never be able to speak normally again.

Now, by the time you read these words I am fully trusting that I will be back to normal and will once again be speaking. But for now—almost silence. A couple of days ago, I was feeling sorry for myself because I have no voice. My voice is my profession and it has been my ministry for nearly fifty years. How do you preach when you can't speak? How do you host a daily radio program with no voice! I was in the "woe is me, I have no voice" mode when suddenly I realized I do have a voice. For now I can't speak with voice, but I certainly can speak through print.

As I sit in God's Waiting Room for my spoken voice to return, God has graciously allowed me to finally speak from my heart the words you are about to read. This book is a simple study of Paul's first letter to the Corinthians. In reality, it's a study of just the first chapter. The book is an epistle, a letter written by the Apostle Paul to one of the most notoriously backslidden churches in history. This church was a total mess. Paul's first words to this sin-ridden, rebellious, carnal, immature congregation have absolutely fascinated me and changed my life. Through Paul's words, I discovered (and so will you):

1. *God's grace is greater than any sin and all of our sins.*
2. *God's grace is a greater motivator to grow, change, improve, and mature than guilt.*
3. *God's grace and sovereignty are greater than any circumstance or enemy you will face.*
4. *God is at work in your life right now whether you can see what He is doing or not.*
5. *God has good plans and a future for your life that is awaiting your surrender.*

Now, read on and take the steps at the end of each chapter to grow deeper in your relationship with Jesus Christ. I pray you will be impacted as I have by these life-changing words: *Grace and peace overflow your life from the Lord Jesus Christ.* In the turmoil, trials, sufferings, confusion, pain, and conflicts surrounding you, you will encounter the Living Christ who will freely give you what you need to be at peace through *remembering whose you are* in every circumstance!

-*Bob Burney*
Columbus, Ohio
Fall, 2012

Chapter One

"THESE PEOPLE ARE SANCTIFIED SAINTS?"

Unto the church of God which is at Corinth, to them that are sanctified in Christ Jesus, called to be saints, with all that in every place call upon the name of Jesus Christ our Lord, both theirs and ours. (1 Corinthians 1:2)

Have you ever been "church shopping"? I know, it's a crude term, but you know what I mean. Most Christians have found themselves looking for a church at one time or another in their lives. Let's say that you've just moved to a new community, and you're looking for that ideal church where you and your family can fellowship. You discover that a new working acquaintance is a fellow follower of Christ with very similar doctrinal beliefs. You're excited at the possibility of visiting his church. Just to get the old ball rolling, you ask your new friend to give you some-one word descriptions of his church. That should give you some idea about the personality and "flavor" before you and the family visit.

He strokes his chin for a moment, breathes a deep breath and says, "Wow, I had never thought of that. Let's see. One word descriptions… hummm. Okay, well, let's see. I guess I would say—

My church is **carnal**,
immature,
and **divided**."

He pauses for another moment or two before continuing and adds, "Uh, we've had an awful lot of **fighting** and **jealousy**. Whoops, that's two words. Hmmm, I guess **rebellious, worldly**. Oh yeah, **sinful**, that's for sure. We've got lots of sin; you could just about name it."

He says with a slight chuckle, "That's about all I can think of right now, does that help?"

You try to hide your total shock and thank your friend for his "help." Now, what are the odds that you will be visiting this man's church this Sunday? Probably, not good. If you are like most of us, we want a church that will help us feel good, get better, and bless us. We want to be around people who will encourage us and lift us up. But, what if we had the perspective that going to church wasn't about what I needed; rather, it was about what they needed?

So now, I have some other questions for you:

Instead of looking for a new church, what if you were somehow chosen to try to bring this sick, deplorable congregation to repentance and revival?
How would you approach them?
What would you say to them?
How would you communicate to them their desperate need to repent and plead for God's forgiveness and mercy?

The Messed Up Church at Corinth

That, my friend, is the background of Paul's first epistle to the church at Corinth. It's named I Corinthians. The church at Corinth fit all of those descriptive words that your "friend" just gave to you for his church. It was one huge mess! Just about every imaginable sin was present within the congregation. In chapter 3, Paul accuses the members of this church of being "bottle babies." He decries that fact that he can't carry on a spiritual conversation because they would choke on the "meat" of the Word. They are still infants sucking on milk in a bottle. He also laments the childish fighting that had erupted about who had led them to Christ. Those WHO had come to Christ under Paul were fighting with those that had come to Christ under Apollos. It's obvious such silly division was deeply hurtful to him.

In chapter four, Paul confesses that their condition is so bad that he is tempted to come to them with a "rod" (vs. 21) but at the same time he expresses his deep love for them. After all this church was his "baby" and had come into existence through his ministry. However, he had never intended for them to remain little children. In chapters five and six he grieves over the reports that he has heard concerning the gross immorality that is present within the body. He catalogues just some of their sin and it is indeed odious.

If you are even a new student to study the Scriptures, I would imagine that none of that is any kind of surprise to you. The condition of the church at Corinth is unmistakable and common knowledge to most Christians. Life-changing truths abound here for you. You may **not** have noticed them before since they are **not** common knowledge. These are what I want you to see.

A few years ago I was reading through my Bible again as I have done many, many times through the years. It would be difficult to tell you how many times I have read through I Corinthians, but this time was different. Do you still have things "jump" off the pages of scripture to you? I hope so! I have been reading my Bible now for over fifty years and I still have those wonderful "eureka" moments when I see something I had never seen before. If you don't have those moments, please ask God to give you some. They are precious and exhilarating. But, of course, you have to be reading your Bible to have them. That's for another book. Anyway, I was reading the first chapter of I Corinthians and as I came through the first nine verses I suddenly stopped in almost shock and disbelief!

Where's the Condemnation?

"Wait a minute! Who is he writing to? Can Paul actually be writing these words to the church at Corinth? I paused for a moment and reflected on what I knew about the spiritual condition of this church, and then I turned again to the text and read the first nine verses another time. I was overwhelmed with something. I was almost incredulous at something I had never seen before.

Paul is writing this letter to a group of immature, carnal, divisive, rebellious Christians and yet these first words reveal none of that! Now, if it were me writing I would have wasted no time at all in taking them to the spiritual woodshed. You see I was raised on good old fashioned "Hell Fire" preaching. By the way God has wonderfully used that preaching through the centuries and still can. It's just that from my background; I learned that spiritually, you call sin, **sin**! You don't make excuses. You don't beat around the bush. You preach truth, condemn sin, and call for repentance. That's all I have ever known and that is not necessarily wrong. But that's not what Paul is doing here (although he certainly does later). I'm praying that God works in you as He did in me to open your eyes to new revelation here in 1 Corinthians that will renew your mind, change your attitudes, and conform you to Christ. With all we've discussed about the condition of Corinth (make sure you fully understand who Paul is writing to and their level of spirituality), I want you to read anew the first nine verses that He writes to them.

> *¹Paul called to be an apostle of Jesus Christ through the will of God, and Sosthenes our brother, ²Unto the church of God which is at Corinth, to them that are sanctified in Christ Jesus, called to be saints, with all that in every place call upon the name of Jesus Christ our Lord, both theirs and ours: ³Grace be unto you, and peace, from God our Father, and from the Lord Jesus Christ.*
>
> *⁴I thank my God always on your behalf, for the grace of God which is given you by Jesus Christ; ⁵That in every thing ye are enriched by him, in all utterance, and in all knowledge; ⁶Even as the testimony of Christ was confirmed in you: ⁷So that ye come behind in no gift; waiting for the coming of our Lord Jesus Christ: ⁸Who shall also confirm you unto the end, that ye may be blameless in the day of our Lord Jesus Christ. ⁹God is faithful, by whom ye were called unto the fellowship of his Son Jesus Christ our Lord.* (1 Corinthians 1:1-9)

Excuse me! Wait a minute! Who is Paul writing to? Does this sound like the congregation we've described? He speaks about and to the Corinthians with words like:

"Sanctified."

"Saints."

"Grace and Peace."

Are you kidding me? Where's the condemnation? Where's the list of sins, the rebuke, and the *fix*? Good grief people, you are a mess; you need to straighten yourselves out! But Paul does just the opposite!

I had never seen this before and to be honest, it rocked my little spiritual world when God was gracious enough to reveal it to me. Paul does not begin with their sins! Isn't that where you and I always begin both with ourselves (self-condemnation) and with others (judgmental and critical)?

Surprisingly, Paul does not begin shouting at them about their failures like we often do. I assure you, Paul does deal with the sin. He doesn't sugar coat it and never ignores it. Later in the letter he gets pretty tough, in fact. It's just not where He begins. As I read those words of Paul in this fresh light, it opened a whole new understanding for me of: **God's incredible grace.** My prayer is that you will experience His grace for you in the same way.

I have been hosting a radio program on WRFD radio in Columbus, Ohio for nearly twenty years; ten years while I was pastoring and now another ten full-time. At the end of every program, I always try to close with these words,

"Remember Whose You Are!"

It's a phrase I used constantly with the young people my wife and I worked with back in another life. I had forgotten it until my sweet wife suggested I use it to close my radio talk show every day and I have done so for nearly twenty years. I sadly admit that I don't always remember just how powerful that challenge really is.

This is exactly what Paul is doing as he writes the introduction to his epistle to Corinth.

He is reminding them of who and *Whose* they are. I have a feeling that if you and I were to be "Judgment Seat Honest," we have far more in common with the people in the church at Corinth than we would like to admit. I know I certainly do. The struggle with the flesh is a constant battle and I often fail. As we begin to look at Paul's words to this miserable flock let's all "remember whose we are."

Reflect and Apply

Take a moment and reflect on what you just read. Be "Judgment Seat Honest" as you answer these questions.

? *If you were chosen to try to bring this sick, deplorable congregation to repentance and revival, how would you approach them?*

? *What would you say to them?*

? *How would you communicate to them their desperate need to repent and plead for God's forgiveness and mercy?*

? *Do you still have things "jump" off the pages of Scripture to you?*

? *How do you respond when you are confronted with your own sin or someone else's? Are your first thoughts of condemnation or grace?*

? *Has reading this chapter changed your mindset, feelings, and attitudes about yourself and others whose lives may be in a mess?*

? *What will you think, feel, and do differently the next time you encounter a Christian or church group who are sinful, carnal, divided, confused, and messed up?*

? *What is your understanding of "belonging" to Christ? Have you ever really meditated on this principle?*

Chapter Two

YOUR POSITION IN CHRIST

Paul called to be an apostle of Jesus Christ through the will of God, and Sosthenes our brother, unto the church of God which is at Corinth, to them that are sanctified in Christ Jesus...." (1 Corinthians 1:1-2 KJV)

Paul's salutation in this epistle (letter) is short and sweet. In verse one he simply asserts his authority as an Apostle and identifies himself as a colleague. He has things to say to these people and he wants to get down to business. It is this business that is amazing! He begins reminding them of a wonderful, precious truth that they had certainly forgotten. In essence he is reminding them that they are **sanctified in position.**

This is obviously something they had not thought about for a long time, but it is the very first truth that Paul wants them to dwell on. He wants them to be reminded of their position in Christ! Notice that this is not a question, it is a proclamation. It is a statement of fact and of truth. These people were "Sanctified in Christ Jesus"—past tense, done deal, finished!

Sanctify, sanctification are not hard words to understand. Sometimes theologians and preachers throw them around like they are mysterious, but in essence it is a very simple principal. To be sanctified simply means to be "set apart" or to be "separated." It also means to be made "pure." So when God sanctifies you, He cleans you up and washes away the dirt, mess, pain, and failures of the past. Your past no longer determines your future. You are set free in Christ to become like Him. The Greek word here is *hagiazo*. It's an extremely important biblical principle. This particular word is used twenty-nine times in twenty-six different verses in the New Testament.

A wonderful way to understand this principle is to take a look backward into the Old Testament and the sacrifices that were offered to God. It was not unusual for lambs to be grown uniquely and exclusively for sacrificial purposes. These lambs were chosen from the rest of the flock because they were the "best of the best." After all, nothing else would be suitable as an appropriate sacrifice to the God of the universe. So, the "best of the best" were **separated from** the rest of the flock. They were **sanctified**. That's exactly what the word means. When it was actually time for a sacrifice to be made you would go to the "best of the best" that had already been **separated from** the rest of the flock and you would pick out the "best of the best" to be offered as a holy sacrifice to God. In other words, the lamb that had been **separated from** was now **separated to** God. The lamb was both **separated from** and **separated to**. That's sanctification in a nutshell!

When a person is born again they are to be both **separated from** the world (2 Corinthians 6:17) and **separated to** God (1 Peter 2:9). Both principles are found throughout the New Testament. In addition to being separated from and to, there are two other aspects of this truth. There is the Progressive aspect and the Positional. One speaks of **Condition**, the other speaks of **Position**.

The Progressive Aspect of Sanctification
This is what we usually hear from the pulpit and read in books. It simply means that today I am to be more like Christ than yesterday (separated from my sinful and self-centered nature and separated to belong to Christ becoming pure, holy, and conformed to His image). Tomorrow I am to be more like Christ than today. It is a process that will continue until we are completely conformed to the image of Christ (Romans 8:29). Obviously, that will continue until we reach Heaven and see Jesus face to face. Day by day we are to become more and more like Jesus and less and less like the depraved and fallen world around us. Where we are in that process obviously changes day to day—sometimes minute by minute. Progress is determined by our obedience and

surrender. Indeed, our condition is constantly changing. While that is solid, biblical truth, I don't believe that is what Paul is referring to here.

The Positional Aspect of Sanctification

It seems clear that Paul is addressing the **positional** aspect of sanctification. He unequivocally states that the Corinthian Christians were "Sanctified in Christ Jesus." From what we know about these people, Paul was certainly **not** referring to their condition. He was reminding them of their position! He was making a proclamation about what Christ had done for them at the moment of their salvation.

When my wife and I were in College the entire campus was familiar with a wonderful, older, faculty member. She had never married and had given her life to serving Christ by teaching. She was known for her deep prayer life, her passion for Christ, but she was also known for a strange habit she had. You see she really liked dessert! At the faculty dining room all of the desserts would be placed on several long tables so they could be quickly served after the entrée had been finished. This precious saint of God would walk into the faculty dining room before the meal and quickly "scope out" all those yummy desserts. When she found one that was particularly to her liking and sweet tooth, she would raise her right forefinger into the air and quickly plunge it into the selected dessert and proclaim with a loud voice, "This one is mine!" Well, having had her finger stuck into it certainly made it hers!

There have been many milestones in my life, but the most important occurred when I was nine years old. I was raised in a wonderful Christian home and some of my earliest memories are from my church in Southern California. I was taught the awesome stories of the Bible from my birth. My pastor was a faithful proclaimer of the truth of God's Word. That didn't make me a Christian any more than sleeping in a garage would make me a car! Although the stories were wonderful and those that told them were sincere, it all didn't click until a Sunday night when I was nine years old. If you promise not to tell anyone, it was a Sunday night service at my church, and I actually slept through most of the sermon.

However, when everyone stood up for the "invitation" something happened deep within me. All that I had heard about being a sinner and that my sin had separated me from God made sense! I was lost.

Even as a nine-year-old boy, the weight of my sin became more than I could bear. The conviction of God's Spirit was overwhelming. I knew I needed to be saved. Fortunately, I had also heard that Jesus Christ had died for me and that He wanted to give me the gift of eternal life if I would simply repent and ask Jesus to save me.

Tears began streaming down my face and I turned to my Dad standing next to me and simply said, "Dad, I want to go."

He knew exactly what I meant and what I needed. He led me forward to an old fashioned altar. My wonderful, red-headed Sunday School teacher, Buster Costa, saw me walk forward and immediately came and knelt on the other side of me. With my father on one side and my Sunday School teacher on the other I prayed a simple, life changing prayer and asked Jesus to be my Savior. At that exact moment, the Holy Spirit of God placed His finger on my heart and proclaimed to the entire universe, "This one is mine!" That was many years ago, but I am still His!

Who You Are In Christ

As you read through Scripture, one of the most glorious phrases you will ever find is "In Christ." There are at least twenty-seven different times that the Word of God proclaims something different about who you are, and what you are "In Christ." All of these and many more describe your position in Christ. Paul is reminding these struggling saints in the Corinthian church of this mighty truth.

Earlier I listed some one word descriptions of the Church at Corinth. It was not a pretty picture! Now, I want you to think of one word descriptions of who **you** are in Christ. What has Christ declared you to be if you have truly trusted Him as Lord and Savior? We could begin with **forgiven**. Scripture clearly says that if you are born again your sins have been put as far away as the East is from the West (Psalm 103:12). They have been cast into the deepest sea (Micah 7:19). Corrie Ten Boom added that God also put up a "No Fishing" sign on that sea as well! Not only have our sins been forgiven but we have been "cleansed from all unrighteousness" (I John 1:9).

Countless Christians have been plagued with "false guilt" because they cannot accept the fact that their sins have really been forgiven. They live in a guilt that is not from God but from the Devil himself. I once counseled a man who was overwhelmed with guilt from something he had done twenty-two years before. I asked him if he had ever asked God to forgive him and his response was, "every day of my life!" He was miserable, defeated, and despondent because he could not believe that God had forgiven him through Christ. Please remember that forgiveness does not always remove consequences.

The God of the universe has already unconditionally accepted you because of Christ!

What about **accepted**? Ephesians 1:6 reveals, "to the praise of the glory of His grace, wherein He hath made us accepted in the Beloved." One of the greatest urges of the human heart is for acceptance. We spend our entire lives trying to be accepted by family, friends, and society. Listen to this incredible news! The God of the universe has already unconditionally accepted you because of Christ!

Acceptance is both a gift of grace we receive and we pass on or "pay it forward." Paul instructs, "Accept one another, then, just as Christ accepted you, in order to bring praise to God (Romans 15:7 NIV)." Acceptance by God empowers us through sanctification to have our deep need for self-worth and significance met in our lives. We can change our inner selves and our behaviors from wrong to right only if we understand that God in Christ truly accepts us. Robert McGee writes, "What a waste to attempt to change behavior without truly understanding the driving needs that cause such behavior! Yet millions of people spend a lifetime searching for love, acceptance, and success without understanding the need that compels them. We must understand that this hunger for self-worth is God-given and can only be satisfied by Him. Our value is not dependent on our ability to earn the fickle acceptance of people, but rather, its true source is the love and acceptance of God. He created us. He alone knows how to fulfill all of our needs."[1]

There is the wonderful truth that in Christ, we have been declared **righteous**. We don't make ourselves "right." The world says, "Get it right. Make it right." God says, "I have made you righteous in Christ."

---

1 Robert S. McGee. *The Search for Significance: Seeing Your True Worth Through God's Eyes* (p. 11). Kindle Edition.

The very righteousness of Christ has been wonderfully "imputed" to us (Romans 4:24). That means it's been handed to us "on a silver platter" without our having to earn it or pay for it. This is one of the most incredible principles found in the New Testament as to our standing in Christ. The Greek word for impute is *logidzomai*. It is often a legal term that implies you are taking something that belongs to one person and "credit" it to someone else's account. Another way to understand it is to study the modern concept of transplantation.

We are wonderfully declared to be righteous by the finished work of Christ.

There is a world of difference between a *pacemaker* and a *transplant*. A pacemaker is a foreign device implanted into a human body. It will never actually become a part of that body, but rather functions within it. A transplant involves an actual part of one body, a living organism that is removed from the donor and placed into the recipient. That living organism that once was a part of one body becomes a living part of another body. Think of this, *the very righteousness of Christ is imputed to you and you are declared righteous because of Christ.* His righteousness, something that is distinctively His, becomes a part of your new nature. We are wonderfully declared to be righteous by the finished work of Christ.

Being declared righteous freely by His grace through the redemption that is in Christ Jesus. (Romans 3:24 emphasis added)

Therefore we conclude that a man is declared righteous by faith without deeds of the law." (Romans 3:28 emphasis added)

Seeing, it is one God, which shall declare righteous the circumcision by faith, and the uncircumcision through faith. (Romans 3:30 emphasis added)

Therefore being declared righteous by faith, we have peace with God through our Lord Jesus Christ. (Romans 5:1 emphasis added)

*Knowing that man is not **declared righteous** by the works of the law but by the faith of Jesus Christ ... not by the works of the law: for by the works of the law shall no person be **declared righteous**.* (Galatians 2:16 emphasis added)

An entire book could be written simply on the subject of what it means to be "In Christ." Rather than trying to give commentary on each of these wonderful truths about being "Sanctified in Christ Jesus," please look at just some of the "In Christ" verses in the New Testament.

In Christ we:

Are Justified: "Being justified freely by his grace through the redemption that is in Christ Jesus" (Romans 3:24).

Have No Condemnation: "There is therefore now no condemnation to them which are in Christ Jesus, who walk not after the flesh, but after the Spirit (Romans 8:1).

Have No Separation: "Nor height, nor depth, nor any other creature, shall be able to separate us from the love of God, which is in Christ Jesus our Lord" (Romans 8:39).

Are One Body: "So we, being many, are one body in Christ, and every one members one of another" (Romans 12:5).

Are Sanctified and Called Saints: "Unto the church of God which is at Corinth, to them that are sanctified in Christ Jesus, called to be saints, with all that in every place call upon the name of Jesus Christ our Lord, both theirs and ours" (1 Corinthians 1:2)

Are Declared Righteous and Made Wise: "But of him are ye in Christ Jesus, who of God is made unto us wisdom, and righteousness, and sanctification, and redemption" (1 Corinthians 1:30). "We are fools for Christ's sake, but ye are wise in Christ; we are weak, but ye are strong; ye are honourable, but we are despised" (1 Corinthians 4:10).

Made Alive: "For as in Adam all die, even so in Christ shall all be made alive" (1 Corinthians 15:22).

Are Established: "Now he which stablisheth us with you in Christ, and hath anointed us, is God" (2 Corinthians 1:21).

Are Triumphant: "Now thanks be unto God, which always causeth us to triumph in Christ, and maketh manifest the savour of his knowledge by us in every place (2 Corinthians 2:14).

Are Enlightened: "But their minds were blinded: for until this day remaineth the same vail untaken away in the reading of the old testament; which vail is done away in Christ" (2 Corinthians 3:13).

Are New Creatures: "Therefore if any man be in Christ, he is a new creature: old things are passed away; behold, all things are become new" (2 Corinthians 5:17). "For in Christ Jesus neither circumcision availeth any thing, nor uncircumcision, but a new creature" (Galatians 6:15).

Are Reconciled: "To wit, that God was in Christ, reconciling the world unto himself, not imputing their trespasses unto them; and hath committed unto us the word of reconciliation" (2 Corinthians 5:19).

Have Liberty: "And that because of false brethren unawares brought in, who came in privily to spy out our liberty which we have in Christ Jesus, that they might bring us into bondage" (Galatians 2:4)

Are Children of God: "For ye are all the children of God by faith in Christ Jesus" (Galatians 3:26).

Are One in Christ: "There is neither Jew nor Greek, there is neither bond nor free, there is neither male nor female: for ye are all one in Christ Jesus" (Galatians 3:28).

Are Blessed With All Spiritual Blessings: "Blessed be the God and Father of our Lord Jesus Christ, who hath blessed us with all spiritual blessings in heavenly places in Christ" (Ephesians 1:3).

Are Seated in Heavenly Places: "And hath raised us up together, and made us sit together in heavenly places in Christ Jesus" (Ephesians 2:6).

Are His Workmanship: "For we are his workmanship, created in Christ Jesus unto good works, which God hath before ordained that we should walk in them" (Ephesians 2:10).

Are Near Jesus: "But now in Christ Jesus ye who sometimes were far off are made nigh by the blood of Christ" (Ephesians 2:13).

Are Made Perfect: "Whom we preach, warning every man, and teaching every man in all wisdom; that we may present every man perfect in Christ Jesus" (Colossians 1:28).

Are Recipients of Faith and Love: "And the grace of our Lord was exceeding abundant with faith and love which is in Christ Jesus" (1 Timothy 1:14).

Are Called to a Holy Calling and Purpose: "Who hath saved us, and called us with an holy calling, not according to our works, but according to his own purpose and grace, which was given us in Christ Jesus before the world began" (2 Timothy 1:9).

That should take your breath away! Think of what honestly happened to you, spiritually, when you were born again!

Your position is totally dependent on the finished work of Christ and therefore it cannot and will not ever change.

Remember the spiritual condition of this church was pathetic. I must admit that there are times that my condition doesn't seem to be much better. If you're honest, that's probably true with you as well.

Let's not forget that Paul struggled with his flesh (Romans 7:15-19). So why does he begin with this strong declaration of their position? Is he ignoring their sin, their failure? Absolutely not, but try to look at it like this. Your **position** is totally dependent on the finished work of Christ; therefore it cannot and will not ever change.

Your **condition** changes day by day, moment by moment. It is constantly changing and is dependent on our obedience to Christ and the circumstances surrounding us. With that in mind I have a couple of questions for you. If you were to meditate 24/7 on your **condition** would your **position** ever change? Of course not. On the other hand, if you truly began to meditate sincerely on your **position** would/could your **condition** change? Absolutely! What do you spend more time thinking about your **condition** or your **position**? If you are the typical Christian, you spend far more time worrying and fretting about your **condition** than meditating on your **position**. Please begin meditating on the "in Christ" verses and you'll never be same. You just might see your condition change.

Once again, Paul is going to deal with the condition of these believers. He will not ignore their sin or failure, but first he powerfully reminds them of Who they are in Christ Jesus.

God not only has a plan for you, He also has a claim on you.

My friend, do you understand that if you are a born again child of God that you are sanctified in Christ Jesus? Do you realize that the God of the Universe has claimed you as His own and that He has set you apart for His service? Do you know that He has a plan for your life and that He is determined to draw you to Himself? Do you understand that everything that is happening in your life at this very moment is part of God's plan to make you like Jesus (Romans 8:28-29)? Someone looking at you might not see that plan. In fact, you might not see that plan either but God does!

God not only has a **plan** for you, He also has a **claim** on you. Later in this epistle Paul asks a very pointed question of the Corinthian Christians. "What? Know ye not that your body is the temple of the Holy Ghost which is in you, which ye have of God, and ye are not your own? For ye are bought with a price: therefore glorify God in your body, and in your spirit, which are God's" (I Corinthians 6:19-20).

It was God who separated and sanctified them. He purchased them with the blood of Christ. They were no longer their own but "bought with a price." In essence Paul was reminding them, "Remember Whose you are!"

Reflect and Apply

Take a moment and reflect on what you just read. Be "Judgment Seat Honest" as you answer these questions.

? *What are some one word descriptions of who you are in Christ?*

? *What has Christ declared you to be in Him?*

? *What does it mean to you that God has forgiven you? Accepted you? Made you righteous in His sight?*

? *If you meditate 24/7 on your* **condition** *would your* **position** *ever change?*

? *If you meditate on your* **position** *would/could your* **condition** *change?*

? *What do you spend more time thinking about your* **condition** *or* **position***?*

? *Do you understand if you're born again you're sanctified in Christ Jesus?*

? *Do you realize the God of the Universe has claimed you as His own?*

? *Do you know that He has set you apart for His service?*

? *Do you know He has a plan for your life and is determined to draw you to Himself?*

? *Do you understand that everything that is happening in your life at this very moment is part of God's plan to make you like Jesus?*

? *How is this going to change the way you look at and live your life?*

Chapter Three

SAINTLY IN PURPOSE

Called to be saints, with all that in every place call upon the name of Jesus Christ our Lord, both their's and our's. (I Corinthians 1:2b)

I couldn't wait to call my wife, Joy, to share the incredible news with her! I had just received an invitation in the mail to the inauguration of President elect George W. Bush. At first I thought it was a hoax, but after doing some research it was the real deal. My wife and I were invited to an all-expense paid trip to our nation's capital to be a part of the inaugural festivities. It was a wonderful time that we will never forget. We had been called and invited to something historic and special.

I hope the church at Corinth had at least some understanding of the awesome invitation that had been extended to them when they were drawn to a personal relationship with Christ. After reminding them that they were **Sanctified in Position,** Paul immediately shares with them that because of a divine invitation from the Creator of the Universe they are called to be saints.

The word "saint" here is a fascinating word in the Greek, *hagios*. No, that's not Haagen Daz! *Hagios* means "most holy thing." The word is used 229 times in the Authorized Version and it is usually translated "holy." The root word is *hagos* which simply means something filled with awe. Now, what makes this particularly interesting is that Paul says the Corinthian Christians were "called to be saints." The Greek word here translated "called" actually means "by divine selection." If we put this all together Paul is literally telling the Corinthians that they have been divinely selected to be something awesome, something holy! If that doesn't bless you, your blesser is busted!

For many years I have heard people moaning and groaning about not knowing what God's purpose for their life is. Well, I've got news! God's purpose for your life is to be a saint! We often think of preaching as being bad news like, *you are a sinner.* While that's true, the good news is that you were created in God's image and He has purposed for you to be a saint. There are, of course, those who teach that you have to die and then wait a few hundred years before some church council declares you to be a saint. That simply is not the teaching of scripture. Sainthood is not determined by your good works and faithfulness but rather it is a result of our salvation in Christ. If there was anyone who did not deserve of sainthood it was this group of believers in the Corinthian church! Just think of the people here that have been "divinely selected" to be something awesomely holy. That means there's hope for me and for you.

My wife and I have a small ministry called CrossPower Ministries. We began the ministry after a wonderful, twenty-five-year pastorate. It was a real step of faith and we promised God that we would go wherever He opened a door regardless of the size of the church inviting us. We had no idea how quickly God would test that commitment. One of the very first meetings we accepted was at a small church plant in a suburb of Cleveland, Ohio. The church was meeting in an old, abandoned restaurant and there were probably a total of fifteen people in the Sunday morning service. The pastor and his wife had about seven children, plus my wife and I—well, you can do the math. It was a very small church!

It came time for the offering and the pastor called two of his sons forward to take up the offering. There were two old baskets sitting on the front row that the boys picked up to use for the offering. I'm not sure I've ever seen such ragged, dirty, worn-out baskets. They were old and filled with holes. I later thought how brilliant this was for the pastor; they wouldn't hold any coins only bills! Anyway, I watched with great curiosity as something absolutely wonderful happened. The pastor prayed for the offering and those boys began passing the baskets. Suddenly, those dirty, filthy, worn out baskets became an instrument of worship of the God of the Universe! After all, our giving is an important part of worship isn't it? We give our offerings not to pay the electric bill of the church or the staff salary. We give because we love God and we worship Him with tithes and offerings. It's been that way since Old Testament times.

That's exactly what Paul is attempting to communicate to the Corinthians. God loves to take the dirty, the vile, and the worthless and transform them into the image of Jesus Christ. He takes the unworthy and makes them worthy of His love. Take a look at the great saints throughout history.

God takes the unworthy and makes them worthy of His love.

Saints of History

David was an adulterer, a murderer, and a liar with a dysfunctional family but God made him a "man after God's own heart" (Acts 13:22). Jacob's name declared him to be a deceiver and a scoundrel and he became one of the fathers of Israel. Abraham was a coward who was willing to give his wife to other men to save his own hide, but after God's wonderful work he became the great patriarch that Sunday School children sing about today. Moses was timid, shy, introverted, and a total failure before God made him an unparalleled leader of leaders. Peter was a traitor and a coward until resurrection power made him the leader of the early church at Pentecost. Timothy was so shy and timid that Paul had to continually encourage him not to quit. And speaking of Paul, let's not forget that he was one of the chief persecutors of the church with a passion for the utter destruction of the early believers.

You simply cannot read the biographies of the great men and women of God through the centuries without being reminded that God always starts with a dirty piece of clay in His hands before He molds a masterpiece of faithfulness and fruitfulness. These Corinthian Christians had incredible potential and they had all been "divinely selected" for holiness—to be Saints! They had, however, forgotten their purpose and their calling. They had become entangled with the world around them. They had become immersed in a culture that was in direct contradiction to their calling in Christ. Can you identify with that? Paul certainly could. You see, Paul also struggled with his flesh just like the Corinthians did.

Paul was probably the most spiritually mature human being that ever walked planet earth other than Jesus Himself, and yet he had a continual, agonizing struggle with his own flesh and the world around him. One of the most encouraging portions of scripture in all of God's word is Romans 7:15-21.

> *For that which I do I allow not: for what I would, that do I not; but what I hate, that do I. If then I do that which I would not, I consent unto the law that it is good. Now then it is no more I that do it, but sin that dwelleth in me. For I know that in me (that is, in my flesh,) dwelleth no good thing: for to will is present with me; but how to perform that which is good I find not. For the good that I would I do not: but the evil which I would not, that I do. Now if I do that I would not, it is no more I that do it, but sin that dwelleth in me. I find then a law, that, when I would do good, evil is present with me.*

Here is the man that God used to write nearly three quarters of the New Testament confessing that he struggles with his flesh. He admits that there is a monster inside of him that contains nothing good. No wonder he is so compassionate with these rascals at Corinth. Maybe we would be more compassionate with our brothers and sisters who are struggling if we would remember the same thing!

Paul is compassionate about the struggles of the Corinthians, but he is not complacent. He is reminding them that they are not living up to their potential in Christ. In essence, he is saying to them, "You **are** saints, now start acting like it! You **are** saints, now start talking like it! You **are** saints, now start thinking like it!" Paul was telling them that they had a heavenly purpose. They were to demonstrate to the world what a saint was like. This was their calling, their Divine invitation. They had been selected for this purpose. They had been chosen to be something awesome for God.

Good, Acceptable, and Perfect Will of God
Paul pleaded with the believers in Rome to surrender to a similar calling in Romans 12:1-2.

I beseech you therefore, brethren, by the mercies of God, that ye present your bodies a living sacrifice, holy, acceptable unto God, which is your reasonable service. And be not conformed to this world: but be ye transformed by the renewing of your mind, that ye may prove what is that good, and acceptable, and perfect, will of God.

He pleads with them to surrender to the calling of God upon their lives. He reasons that this is their "reasonable service." Notice the emphasis Paul puts on surrender. Their bodies are to be given to God as a daily, living sacrifice, and their minds were to be surrendered to God's truth rather than allowing the world to squeeze them into its ugly mold. In essence it all came down to decisions. The Romans Paul was writing to could choose what and to whom they surrendered to on a daily basis. They could choose to reject the world around them and its mold, and choose to set their minds on the things of Christ which was God's good, acceptable, and perfect will.

Are you willing to surrender your will and ways to God? The story is told of a preacher giving a call to young people to go to the mission field. One young man responded, "I'm not willing to go." The preacher responded, "Let me ask you then, *are you willing to be made willing.*" You have a choice to make and that choice begins with surrendering your own self-centered will to God. Once that is done, a saint begins to discover that every future righteous decision isn't a struggle of will. Rather, doing what's right is a joyful, immediate yielding to God's will because one's free will has already been set aside, i.e. sanctified.

In like manner the Corinthians could make choices. When the letter was written it was obvious that the choices they had made were not in line with God's will. They had been corrupted by the world and the world system. They had chosen to fight with each other and display a decidedly un-Christ-like character. They had chosen to reject their calling. The world around them was not seeing a group of saints bringing glory to Christ, but rather a bunch of carnal children bringing reproach to Christ. I believe that Paul is hoping that they have simply forgotten whose they were. He is trusting that once they are reminded of the fact they have been purchased with the precious blood of Christ and that they have been redeemed from the corruption of the world, they will return in repentance to the supremacy of Christ's claim on their lives and once again demonstrate to the world what a saint is like.

[call out] **The problem is never God's power or provision – the problem is always our surrender.**

God loves to take the dirty, the vile, the weak, and the useless and transform them into something awesome for His glory. In fact, only the dirty, the vile, the weak, and the useless qualify for His Grace. Later in this first chapter Paul reveals the kind of people that God normally uses.

> *[26] For ye see your calling, brethren, how that not many wise men after the flesh, not many mighty, not many noble, are called: [27] But God hath chosen the foolish things of the world to confound the wise; and God hath chosen the weak things of the world to confound the things which are mighty; [28] And base things of the world, and things which are despised, hath God chosen, yea, and things which are not, to bring to nought things that are: [29] That no flesh should glory in his presence.* (1 Corinthians 1:26-29)

Yes, these are the kinds of people that God calls to be Saints! The weak, foolish, despised, and base are the ones that God transforms into something awesome! Like those offering baskets, God takes the ordinary, the dirty, and the rejected and fills them with His Spirit and transforms them into instruments of worship to the God of creation.

If you have been born again, this is your calling, your purpose. The question is will you surrender to that purpose? Will you allow Him to conform you to His image (Romans 8:29). Will you allow Him to make you all He wants you to be? The problem is never God's power or provision – the problem is always our surrender. Today, will you

Remember Whose You Are?

Reflect and Apply

Take a moment and reflect on what you just read. Be "Judgment Seat Honest" as you answer these questions.

? *Have you, like the Corinthians, forgotten your purpose and calling?*

? *Have you become entangled with the world around you?*

? *Have you become immersed in a culture that was in direct contra-diction to your calling in Christ?*

? *Are you living up to your potential in Christ?*

? *Are you acting like, talking like, and thinking like saints?*

? *Will you surrender to God's purpose?*

? *Will you allow Him to conform you to His image?*

? *Will you allow Him to make you all He wants you to be?*

Chapter Four

SUFFICIENT IN POWER

Grace be unto you, and peace, from God our Father, and from the Lord Jesus Christ. I thank my God always on your behalf, for the grace of God which is given you by Jesus Christ; That in every thing ye are enriched by him, in all utterance, and in all knowledge; Even as the testimony of Christ was confirmed in you: So that ye come behind in no gift; waiting for the coming of our Lord Jesus Christ. (1 Corinthians 1:3-7)

I grew up in Southern California and I grew up loving cars—a good combination! A very fond childhood memory was going to the Model T races at a place called Signal Hill. Signal Hill was a somewhat famous area close to the city of Long Beach. Oil was discovered there sometime in the late 40s or 50s and the entire top of the hill was dotted with those oil wells that looked like rocking horses as they rocked up and down bringing oil to the surface from the depths below. The "hill" rose high above the Long Beach area and on one side there was the steepest road I have ever seen. I have no idea what the exact percentage of grade was, but for this little guy it looked like you were climbing straight up a wall. When you drove up its incline and then turned around to go back down, it would put your stomach right into your mouth.

Every year a local club would host the Model T races. You're probably somewhat familiar with the old Ford Model T's from the early 1900s. They were great cars, but compared to today's vehicles they were pathetically small in horsepower. Large crowds would gather along the hill and watch the old "horseless carriages" trudge up the formidable hill before them. Many made it to the top, but many did not. It was not unusual to see an old "Tin Lizzy" start valiantly up the hill only to stop mid-way, often with the radiator steaming, and then slowly back down the hill with the brakes smoking.

Several years later when I was back in Southern California from College, I decided to go visit "the Hill" again. I had a powder blue Ford Galaxie 500 XL with a high powered V-8 engine. I approached the bottom of the hill and floored my blue rocket. The steep incline that I had seen conquer so many of the Model T's was no match for the 400 horses under my hood. The hill was the same; it was all a matter of how much power was available!

The hill was the same; it was all a matter of how much power was available!

In 1 Corinthians, Paul is writing to a group of people that have been overcome by some of the high hills of life. Their lives had shuddered and shaken to a stop by the hills of sin, self, and compromise. Their spiritual radiators were steaming and they had lost the ability to overcome the trials of daily life. In a very powerful way, Paul reminds them that they are **Sufficient in Power.**

After reminding them that they are **Sanctified in Position** and that they are **Saintly in Purpose,** Paul immediately assures them that their pathetic spiritual life is **not** because they are lacking in the power that God that has available to them. Indeed, he assures them that God has given them sufficient power to live a victorious, overcoming Christian life. They already possess everything they need! It was part of the "package" when they were born-again. Before being saved, we have the knowledge of good and evil. We know what's right and wrong, but we simply lack the power to always choose the right and do it. A saint has the knowledge and the power to do what's right and good. In fact, since the saint is being conformed to Christ's image, the first instinct or motivation is to do what's right, to purpose to live out God's will no matter what the cost or sacrifice!

Grace and Peace

He first draws their attention to the grace and peace from "God our Father, and from the Lord Jesus Christ." Have you ever thought about how powerful grace is? Think about how man has harnessed the power of the atom. The power of an atomic weapon is totally mind boggling. Just a few of these powerful weapons could wipe out huge portions of the population of the earth. The atom has also been tamed to bring us energy. Millions of homes are powered by relatively small amounts of radioactive material.

Yet man has never been able to harness the compulsions of the human heart. The best and brightest minds in psychology, psychiatry, and sociology struggle constantly to "cure" the addict, the criminal, and the carouser with little success. If man had the "answer" to the problem of the human heart we would have no prisons. There would be no need for jails, police, and the courts. Yet, there are countless stories of men and women whom the world system has tried to cure to no avail.

Then they came face to face with God's grace. Hopeless drunks, pathetic addicts, and washed up convicts are transformed by the power of God's grace. There is no limit to what the grace of God can do when unleashed in a life and accepted by faith. How much of that grace was available to the Corinthians? All they needed. There is a limitless supply. You may be convinced that you are not worthy of God's grace. That's the good news to the Corinthians and to you! No one is worthy! If you were worthy, you wouldn't need it. If you could earn it, it wouldn't be grace any longer. Grace is receiving God's **R**iches **A**t **C**hrist's **E**xpense. It cost you nothing to receive it, but it cost Him everything to give it. This principle, this power is so important that Paul reminds them twice that this wonderful grace is a gift from Jesus Himself to all who believe. It is a gift more powerful than all of man's effort, intellect, and wisdom. It is yours from Jesus Himself.

G.R.A.C.E. is receiving God's **R**iches **A**t **C**hrist's **E**xpense.

Paul continues this thought in **2 Corinthians 9:8, "And God is able to make all grace abound toward you; that ye, always having all sufficiency in all things, may abound to every good work."** Did you catch that? Here is a formula for a powerful, victorious life. God gives you His grace and makes it "abound" toward you which gives you all the sufficiency you need. He is not speaking from theory either. At the very end of his second epistle to this church, Paul shares what was probably the most difficult time of his life—his "thorn in the flesh." We have little idea what it was except that Paul thought it was going to kill him and he begged God to remove it.

And lest I should be exalted above measure through the abundance of the revelations, there was given to me a thorn in the flesh, the messenger of Satan to buffet me, lest I should be exalted above measure. For this thing I besought the Lord thrice, that it might depart from me. (2 Corinthians 12:7-8)

Paul is convinced he's "going down for the third time" and cries out to God for deliverance, for strength, and for power to overcome this horrible experience. What does God do?

And he said unto me, My grace is sufficient for thee: for my strength is made perfect in weakness. Most gladly therefore will I rather glory in my infirmities, that the power of Christ may rest upon me. (2 Corinthians 12:9)

God gives Paul all the grace he needs which God says is "sufficient." We usually have it backwards. We are convinced that we have to become "strong." That's what the world tells us. The world despises weakness. God loves it. In fact, God often sends or allows circumstances, difficult people, sickness, and tragedy to strip us of our strength, our pride, and our own sufficiency so we can accept His power and His sufficiency. In the powerful passage in 2 Corinthians 12:10, Paul summarized this by saying, "Therefore I take pleasure in infirmities, in reproaches, in necessities, in persecutions, in distresses for Christ's sake: for when I am weak, then am I strong."

Paul admits, reluctantly, that as long as he was strong he would never find Christ's strength. It was only after he was "buffeted" that he was ready to accept God's grace as his sufficiency (2 Corinthians 12:7). This word "buffet" here is extremely interesting. It means to beat violently with a fist. It is used for the beating that Jesus suffered in Matthew 26:67 and Mark 14:65. The implication is that Paul was "beaten to a pulp" by this thorn in the flesh.

Do you remember where this "gift" came from? It was from God Himself. What was the purpose of this gift? To make Paul as weak as someone who has just gotten the beating of their life. The result is that Paul begins to live his life in the sufficiency of God's grace. As a result Paul was used of God to write nearly three quarters of the New Testament, and was responsible for bringing thousands to Christ while establishing the modern mission's movement.

Learn this lesson: God is sufficient, you are not! Your arms are much too short to box with God.

Have you considered the possibility that the circumstances that you have faced or possibly are facing right now have been designed by God to bring you to a place of "weakness"? Have you ever felt like a human punching bag and that God has forsaken you? He has not forsaken you. He's preparing you to receive a mega-dose of His sufficient grace which produces His Peace. But you'll never see the sufficiency of His grace as long as you are doing things in your own strength. Maybe it's time to stop fighting and surrender. Someone once said, "Your arms are much too short to box with God." Learn this lesson: He is sufficient, you are not!

All of God's riches; all of the power, grace, blessing, indwelling, and filling that is available had been given to us.

Enriched in all Utterance and Knowledge

That in everything ye are enriched by him, in all utterance, and in all knowledge. (1 Corinthians 1:5)

Paul continues to remind the Corinthians what is available to them for life's daily struggles. It is not unusual for this verse to be skipped over in many commentaries but it should not be. There is some extraordinarily exciting truth to be learned in this verse. Paul has just driven home the point that these struggling Christians had been given the transforming power of God's grace and now he turns their attention to the power of God's Spirit. He declares that "in everything" they are enriched. You and I are prone at times to exaggerate but God does not. If Paul, under the direction of the Holy Spirit, says everything, he means exactly that. All of God's riches have been poured out on them. All of the power, grace, blessing, indwelling, and filling of God's Spirit that is available had been given to them. They had been made rich or enriched in **everything** by Christ through the Holy Spirit.

If you know Christ as your Savior and have been born-again, then right here, right now you possess everything you need to lead an overcoming, victorious Christian life.

Then Paul draws attention to specifics saying "all utterance" and "all knowledge." There is some controversy if you read a group of commentaries on what the "utterance" means. Most believe it deals with speech, since the Greek word is *logos* while a few believe it deals specifically with doctrine and even believe that utterance should have been translated "doctrine." Some even believe it is a reference to the ability that God had given some in the church to speak in other languages (I Corinthians 14). I won't try to give a definitive answer and I'll leave that up to the commentators, but I do believe that when you put "utterance" (*logos* = word) together with "all knowledge" you have to conclude that this is a fulfillment of what Jesus said in John 14. Jesus promised His followers that after His departure He would send the Holy Spirit who would be "the Spirit of truth" (John 14:17). Furthermore, when the Holy Spirit came, "He shall teach you **all** things" (John 14:26 emphasis mine). Wow! The indwelling Spirit of God would become the ultimate teacher.

I hear people constantly declaring that they can't understand the Bible. I wonder how many of them actually depend on the Holy Spirit to teach them? I am absolutely convinced that God's children approach scripture with a defeatist attitude and an assumption that the Bible is not understandable, not comprehensible and ignore the promise that Jesus made concerning the teaching ministry of the Holy Spirit. Now, I admit that the Word of God is infinite in its truth and if we spent every moment of every day studying it, we still would not plumb the depths of its wisdom. But I also believe that God will teach us daily what we need to know and must know to face life's daily trials. Think of the fact that the One who wrote scripture is the continual indwelling presence in our hearts! Our study of scripture would change dramatically if we actually expected God, through His Spirit, to enlighten us when we read and study it.

God will teach us daily what we need to know and must know to face life's daily trials.

I believe this is the message Paul is addressing with the Corinthians. They had been given the Holy Spirit and had been enriched by Christ with the *Logos* given by the Holy Spirit. All knowledge had been made available to them through the work, ministry, and indwelling of the Holy Spirit. **They were not deficient in knowledge or power; they were deficient in faith and obedience.** It was not a lack of God's power that plunged them into carnality and immaturity. It was their own refusal to avail themselves of what God had provided to them, either through ignorance or rebellion. In either case their failure was not a result of any deficiency in what was provided to them as followers of Christ.

Spiritual Millionaires

I want you to think seriously about the fact that if you know Christ as your Savior and have been born-again, then right here, right now you possess everything you need to lead an overcoming, victorious Christian life. You have been given God's Spirit to comfort you, to instruct you, and to convict you. You have been given God's Word (*Logos*) which brought the universe into existence. You have the Son who gave Himself for you at Calvary and now sits on the right hand of the Father to intercede for you. You have the Father who pities (deep, compassionate understanding Psalm 103:13-14) you and draws you to Himself.

If all of this is true, then how could these Corinthian Christians be living as spiritual paupers, when in reality they were millionaires? I'm reminded of a story about the son of an Arab Sheik. The Father was worth billions because of his oil holdings. The son went into a downward spiral of rebellion and left his home to travel to America. His life was marked by drugs, alcohol, and women. He soon wasted everything and became homeless in New York City. His existence was pathetic and destitute.

Many years passed and the son spent them all in meaningless endeavors of futility and wantonness. Unknown to the son, his father died with the son being the only heir. The estate of the billionaire hired several investigators to attempt to find the wayward son. For over a decade the hired investigators scoured the planet looking for the heir.

One fateful, winter day a tall man in an expensive suit approached a shell of a man lying on a lonely sidewalk in New York. The son had been found! After making a positive identification, the professional investigator informed the homeless vagabond of his father's death and that he was indeed the heir to a vast fortune that had been his for many years without him knowing it. A billionaire had been living in the gutter unaware of the wealth available to him. He had cut himself off from untold riches due to his rebellion and ignorance.

My friend, you are an heir of God and a "joint heir with Jesus Christ" (Romans 8:17). All the riches of Christ are yours. "Blessed *be* the God and Father of our Lord Jesus Christ, who hath blessed us with all spiritual blessings in heavenly *places* in Christ:" (Ephesians 1:3). How many "spiritual blessings" are yours? All of them!

The real question is do you believe that? The Corinthians certainly didn't before they received this letter and there's a good chance you don't either. It's a faith thing. All of those riches were available to the Corinthians and they are available to you **today**. But they will be worthless unless claimed by faith.

Reflect and Apply

Take a moment and reflect on what you just read. Be "Judgment Seat Honest" as you answer these questions.

? *Have you ever thought about how powerful grace is?*
? *What is God's formula for a powerful, victorious life?*
? *Have you considered the possibility that the circumstances that you are facing have been designed by God to bring you to a place of "weakness"?*
? *Have you ever felt like a human punching bag and God has forsaken you?*
? *Are you living as a spiritual pauper instead of a millionaire?*
? *How many "spiritual blessings" are yours?*

Chapter Five

SUFFICIENT TO LIVE IN VICTORY

Who shall also confirm you unto the end, that ye may be blameless in the day of our Lord Jesus Christ. (1 Corinthians 1:8)

Have you ever thought about what kept the children of Israel out of their "promised land" of victory that flowed with milk and honey? The land had been promised to Abraham some 450 years before. Well, that's easy, you might say. The land was filled with giants, walled cities, brutal enemies, and superior armies. You could conclude that the opposition was just too great and the circumstances were just too overwhelming. You could easily come to that conclusion, but you would be absolutely wrong. The writer of the book of Hebrews tells us the surprising truth.

But with whom was he grieved forty years? Was it not with them that had sinned, whose carcasses fell in the wilderness? And to whom sware he that they should not enter into his rest, but to them that believed not? So we see that they could not enter in because of unbelief. (Hebrews 3:17-19)

What, it wasn't the giants, the walled cities or the overwhelming odds against them? No, it was the fact that they were not willing to believe God and His promises. They were looking at the size of the giants rather than the size of God! God had promised them this land and He would be their resource in conquering it. The sad turning point was when twelve spies were sent into the land to scope it out. When they returned, they confirmed that it was everything that God had said it was. It was beautiful, fertile, plentiful, and God said it was theirs for the claiming. So, did they cross the Jordan River and possess this incredible land? Not exactly. Out of the twelve spies only two saw God, the rest saw giants.

> *But the men that went up with him said, We be not able to go up against the people; for they are stronger than we. And they brought up an evil report of the land which they had searched unto the children of Israel, saying, The land, through which we have gone to search it, is a land that eateth up the inhabitants thereof; and all the people that we saw in it are men of a great stature. And there we saw the giants, the sons of Anak, which come of the giants: and we were in our own sight as grasshoppers, and so we were in their sight. And all the congregation lifted up their voice, and cried; and the people wept that night.* (Numbers 13:31-14:1)

Can you grasp what is happening here? For 450 years Israel has prayed, dreamed, and wept for the land of Canaan promised to their Father Abraham. They are finally here! They are literally standing a few yards from their God-given possession and what are they doing? They're weeping and wailing because of an "evil report" of God's promised land. The result was that an entire generation travelled around in circles through the wilderness and never experienced what God had prepared for them. They had been delivered from the bondage of Egypt by the blood of lambs. Pharaoh's power had been broken at the Red Sea. They had been given everything they needed to conquer their enemies and to live in wonderful victory in a beautiful land, but they chose to put their eyes on circumstances rather than the promises and provision of God. They simply did not believe God.

The child of God has become victorious over the power of sin because of his identification with Christ's finished work on the Cross.

49

Freedom from the Bondage of Sin

Paul assured the Corinthians they could achieve a place where they would be found blameless in the day of our Lord Jesus. How could this be? It is because victory is not dependent on what you do. It is dependent on what He has done! But remember—it's a **faith** thing. My dear friend, I want you to think through this seriously. If you have been born-again, then you have been set free from the bondage of sin by the blood of the Lamb. Read what Paul says to the Roman Christians.

Knowing this, that our old man is crucified with him, that the body of sin might be destroyed, that henceforth we should not serve sin. For he that is dead is freed from sin. (Romans 6:6-7)

The child of God has become victorious over the power of sin because of his identification with Christ's finished work on the Cross. That truth is communicated beautifully in Paul's letter to the Galatians.

I am crucified with Christ: nevertheless I live; yet not I, but Christ liveth in me: and the life which I now live in the flesh I live by the faith of the Son of God, who loved me, and gave himself for me. (Galatians 2:20)

There is a promised land reserved for you and I'm not talking about Heaven (although that certainly awaits us). Many people are convinced that the Land of Heaven is a biblical type of Heaven. In fact, there have been hundreds, possibly thousands of songs that make that connection. We've all heard songs and sermons about one day crossing over "chilly Jordan" into that "Heavenly Promised Land." Well, I'm really sorry to ruin all those songs for you, but think for a moment. Why didn't the children of Israel cross over Jordan? They saw giants, walled cities, and enemies. They refused to believe God for their victory over those obstacles.

If Canaan is a representation of Heaven, then who are the Giants in Heaven? Who are the enemies that we will have to battle once we cross over "chilly Jordan" like the songs say? Canaan simply cannot represent Heaven. It just doesn't fit! Then what does it represent? That's actually pretty easy. It's the victorious Christian life promised to every follower of Christ. If you have lived on this planet for any length of time at all after you were saved, then you know that this world is filled with giants of every kind and enemies aplenty. There's a very good chance that as you read these words there are some giants that you're dealing with and certainly some enemies that are trying to trip you up in your Christian life. But, here's the wonderful truth, God has provided all you need to have victory over every one of them.

Do you think God knew about the giants and walled cities in Canaan? I kind of think He did and yet He boldly told the children of Israel to march right into the middle of them. He promised them, that if they would go into the land by faith, that He would provide them with everything they needed to be victorious over any and all of their enemies. Read it for yourself.

Then will the LORD drive out all these nations from before you, and ye shall possess greater nations and mightier than yourselves. Every place whereon the soles of your feet shall tread shall be yours: from the wilderness and Lebanon, from the river, the river Euphrates, even unto the uttermost sea shall your coast be. There shall no man be able to stand before you: for the LORD your God shall lay the fear of you and the dread of you upon all the land that ye shall tread upon, as he hath said unto you. (Deuteronomy 11:23-25)

Pretty clear isn't it? God said, you go by faith and I'll do the rest. Did they believe and obey God? Not at all and the consequences resulted in defeat, despair, and misery. Sounds like a lot of Christians I know. They're saved, born-again, on their way to Heaven but miserable, defeated, and filled with despair.

In reality, the pagans in Canaan had more belief in the power of Israel's God than Israel did!

Now, since we've travelled in our literary time machine back to the days of the children of Israel in the wilderness, let's push a couple of buttons and fast forward forty years. When we open the door an entire generation of God's people have perished in the desert and a new generation with a new leader is standing on the brink of the Jordan once again. Again spies are sent into the land of Canaan. This time, however, with quite different results. The spies stop off at one of the largest and most fortified cities in the land, Jericho. God leads them to, of all people, a prostitute who possibly ran a brothel up on the wall of the city. If you haven't read the story lately, you should, it's absolutely fascinating. The prostitute's name is Rahab and by God's grace, He uses her to hide the spies from the men of Jericho. Here is the part of the story that totally blows my mind.

> *And she said unto the men, I know that the LORD hath given you the land, and that your terror is fallen upon us, and that all the inhabitants of the land faint because of you. For we have heard how the LORD dried up the water of the Red sea for you, when ye came out of Egypt; and what ye did unto the two kings of the Amorites, that were on the other side Jordan, Sihon and Og, whom ye utterly destroyed. And as soon as we had heard these things, our hearts did melt, neither did there remain any more courage in any man, because of you: for the LORD your God, he is God in heaven above, and in earth beneath.* (Joshua 2:9-11)

Remember, this is forty years after the first group of spies came into the land and brought back an "evil report." This is forty years after the Red Sea. Rahab is telling these men that the enemies of Israel have been shaking in their sandals for forty years! In reality, the pagans in Canaan had more belief in the power of Israel's God than Israel did! The pagans feared God and God's people feared the pagans. There's something terribly wrong with that picture. I'm convinced that if the children of Israel had believed God and obeyed Him as He instructed them to do, they could have marched into Canaan and their enemies would have laid down their weapons at their feet out of pure fear and terror. Their downfall came because of unbelief, not their enemies. God had promised them victory over every enemy in every battle as long as they fought those battles in God's way, not their own. When they fought in the power of His might and strength, they were victorious. When they fought in their own strength, they were defeated. Sometime take a look at the difference between the battles of Jericho and Ai.

- *What giants are you facing right now?*
- *What habits, attitudes, and difficult people seem to be keeping you from your promised land?*
- *Are you walking in spiritual circles in a desert wilderness of defeat, despair, and misery?*

Allow me to remind you that living for Christ is a faith thing. Right here, right now, you possess all you need to walk in victory. You didn't get saved on the value menu hoping to biggie size your salvation later. Take a moment and meditate on what Paul says in Ephesians 3:19-21.

And to know the love of Christ, which passeth knowledge, that ye might be filled with all the fullness of God. Now unto him that is able to do exceeding abundantly above all that we ask or think, according to the power that worketh in us, unto him be glory in the church by Christ Jesus throughout all ages, world without end. Amen.

Because of Christ's finished work on the cross, all Christians are already filled with "all the fullness of God." And because of that there is a power working in you that is able to do things you never dreamed of.

For in him dwelleth all the fullness of the Godhead bodily. And ye are complete in him, which is the head of all principality and power. (Colossians 2:9-10)

All the fullness of God dwells in Jesus and "ye are complete in him." It's very possible that you simply don't believe that you can live in victory. So many Christians see themselves as victims instead of victors. When faced with a problem or painful circumstance, they expect the worse, anticipate failure, and believe the lies of the Devil. What are they? When God asks you to obey, instead of trusting Him for the power, strength and resources to accomplish the good work He calls you to do, do you find yourself listening to the enemy's lies:

You don't have the smarts or the strength to do that.
You don't have the time.

You don't have enough money or resources.
You don't have the support of others; you're all alone.
Even if you did it, it wouldn't make any difference at all.

Stop believing the lies; believe and trust the truth of God. You are a victor not a victim.

The Corinthians certainly didn't and Paul had to give them a stern reminder of their resources in Christ. He assured them that their failures were not God's fault. Is God trying to teach you the same lesson? My precious friend, if you are a born-again, blood washed follower of Christ then you are a spiritual millionaire. Just like the Corinthians, you are sufficient in power and sufficient to live in victory, but it's a faith thing. Possibly you, too, need to be reminded: **Whose you are.**

Reflect and Apply

Take a moment and reflect on what you just read. Be "Judgment Seat Honest" as you answer these questions.

? *Have you been living a miserable, defeated life filled with despair?*
? *What giants are you facing in your life right now?*
? *What habits, attitudes, and difficult people seem to be keeping you from your promised land?*
? *Are you walking in spiritual circles in a desert wilderness of defeat, despair and misery?*
? *Are you born-again?*
? *Do you know that you have been set free from the bondage of sin by the blood of the Lamb?*
? *Are you a child of God?*
? *Do you know you have the sufficiency to become victorious over the power of sin because of Christ's finished work on the cross?*
? *Is your victory dependent on what you do?*
? *What is your victory dependent on?*

Chapter Six

SEALED IN PROVIDENCE

So that ye come behind in no gift; waiting for the coming of our Lord Jesus Christ: Who shall also confirm you unto the end, that ye may be blameless in the day of our Lord Jesus Christ. God is faithful, by whom ye were called unto the fellowship of his Son Jesus Christ our Lord. (1 Corinthians 1:7-9)

I hate to be late! It just absolutely drives me crazy to be late to anything. I'm one of those people that would rather be thirty minutes early than three minutes late. This is just one of many of my personal "quirks." It has often caused stress in my family and marriage as I get antsy and at times agitated when it looks like my punctuality is threatened. Many years ago when our children were young, we planned a vacation trip from Ohio to Florida. As most families do, we had set a specific time that we wanted to leave on the trip. We had calculated how long we would drive between stops and an approximate arrival time at our destination. The day of departure was, well, one of "those days." Everything that could go wrong did and it was clear that we would not be leaving at our pre-arranged time.

I was getting antsy and agitated as the minutes passed the pre-ordained blast off, I started to say things like, "This is going to ruin the plan! We're not going to make to where we wanted to have lunch! The traffic in Atlanta is going to be horrible by the time we get there!"

I'm huffing and puffing around the house trying to get the car packed and everyone out the front door. We finally got in the car and started the journey. It was not a pleasant start. I'm trying to keep my cool but underneath, I'm fuming. There was an odd silence in the car as everyone tried to avoid the Dad Volcano that would occasionally erupt. After driving a few hours we suddenly saw that all traffic had stopped on the Interstate. A horrific accident had occurred a short time before and emergency vehicles were everywhere assisting the victims in the midst of the carnage. We never heard the full details, but it was clear that there were fatalities.

My wife and I looked at each other in stunned silence as we both realized at the same moment, there was the possibility that if we had left our home "on time" we could very well have been involved in the accident. Was our delay in leaving God's special Providence? Did God supernaturally protect us from harm, injury or even worse? Of course, we will not know until we get to Heaven, but my frustration about the late departure went away very quickly as we breathed a prayer for the victims of the crash and thanked God for our safety. I'm certain that most of you reading these words could offer similar testimonies where God has used disappointments, delays, and "mistakes" to bring about His special plan in your life and that of your family.

What incredibly encouraging words Paul used in the opening verses of his letter to the Corinthians! "Waiting for the coming of our Lord Jesus Christ," "Confirm you unto the end," "blameless in the day of our Lord Jesus Christ," and "God is faithful." All of these phrases must have given the Corinthian Christians great encouragement. While they were waiting for Jesus, He would confirm them all the way unto the end so they would be blameless when He returns. All because God is faithful!

Was all of this true? Absolutely, although it certainly did not look like it at the time these words were written. When this letter was written these people were pathetic in their walk, weak in their faith, immature in their spirit, divided in their relationships, and sinful in their habits. We know, however, from reading Paul's second letter to the church at Corinth that a wonderful spiritual renewal occurred—so much so that Paul almost apologizes for writing the first letter where he severely rebukes them for their sin.

What happened between the time Paul wrote the first and when he wrote second letters to the Corinthians? "God is faithful," that's what happened. Yes, the Corinthians turned from their sin and they repented.

Yes, they dealt with the sin in the church, but it was all because of God's faithfulness to them in convicting them of their sin and bringing circumstances into their life and church (including Paul's first letter) that brought them to repentance. It is not my desire or intent to launch into a theological treatise on the Providence of God. I'll allow the theologians and professors to do that. It is my desire, however, to assure you that the hand of God is constantly upon His children and it is impossible to hide from His eye or His presence.

David certainly understood this truth when he wrote Psalm 139:7-12. He clearly tells us that there is no place we can hide from an Omnipresent God. If I go up, He's there. If I go down, He's there. He's in the sea, and He's in the sky. He's in the light and He's in the dark. Even in my mother's womb, God was there. He's everywhere and there is nowhere to hide from Him! At times that truth brought great comfort of David. At other times it must have brought great anguish. God was always there and David's life is a startling illustration of that truth.

God's "A to B" Plan

In fact, Scripture is literally saturated with this wonderful principle that God has a plan and He is constantly working out that plan in your life even when you don't even realize it. I call it the "A to B Plan." Here's how it works. When you accept Christ as Savior you are at the start of God's plan which we'll call point "A." God has an ultimate destiny and destination for you which we'll call point "B." There is much between point A and point B. So if point A is salvation, what is point B? It's becoming like Jesus. That's God's ultimate plan for you. Everything in between is ultimately irrelevant in the light of eternity. You have an occupation or a vocation. You may or may not have a spouse and family. You may have a particular educational history or none. You may be at the top of the economic scale or at the bottom. That's all rather meaningless compared to God's ultimate goal for you which is to become like Jesus Christ. Christ indwells you. Your every thought, word, feeling, motivation, attitude, and action embodies and incarnates His Spirit. You are being transformed and conformed to His image. Do others see Him in all you are and do?

I don't know how much you have accomplished in your profession or your field of endeavor, but I somehow doubt that the God who created the universe is very impressed. How much money would you have to make to impress God? See what I mean?

You see, I know God's plan for your life. Oh, I don't know all the details, I just know the end. One of the most familiar verses in the Bible is Romans 8:28

And we know that all things work together for good to them that love God, to them who are the called according to his purpose.

It's very possible that you can quote that verse from memory. It's rare, however, that anyone can quote the next verse. That's strange, because while millions have claimed the promise of Romans 8:28, it is absolutely meaningless without the conditions of verse 29.

*For whom he did foreknow, he also did predestinate to be **conformed to the image** of his Son, that he might be the firstborn among many brethren.* (emphasis added)

Here is the powerful truth. All Christians have been predestined to become like Jesus. For centuries there has been the contentious debate about "election," "predestination," etc. That's not the subject here. This is not a statement about Calvinism or any other "ism." It's a simple, straightforward pronouncement of God's plan for every Christian who is living or has ever lived. We have all been predestined to be "conformed to the image of His son." We're supposed to become just like Christ. Now, how does God accomplish that? Verse twenty-eight says God uses all things to accomplish this.

God has a plan to get you from Point A to Point B and if you surrender to that plan, He'll put everything together to accomplish that purpose. Scripture is filled with illustrations of this principle where God takes someone where they are and throughout their life works out His plan. The strange thing is that His plan is hardly ever anything like our plan. In fact, often His plan does all kinds of terrible things to our plan. At times it is very difficult to even see His plan, but I assure you it's there. Let's take a look at some Bible stories where God took His people from Point A to Point B. Remember, Point A is where God finds them – Point B is where He ultimately wants to take them. There's a whole lot in between and some of it ain't pretty!

God has a plan to get you from Point A to Point B and if you surrender to that plan, He'll put everything together to accomplish that purpose.

Jacob

The life of Jacob is truly one of the stranger "heroes" of the Bible. He came from an incredibly dysfunctional home with an over protective mother and a disengaged father. His story is proof that God can and does use "all things" in our development for His service. Jacob's "entrance" into this world was accompanied by an unusual promise—his **Point A.** Rebekah, his mother, was barren until her husband Isaac pleaded with God to open her womb. Not only did God answer Isaac's prayer, He answered with twins!

> *And the children struggled together within her; and she said, If it be so, why am I thus? And she went to enquire of the LORD. And the LORD said unto her, Two nations are in thy womb, and two manner of people shall be separated from thy bowels; and the one people shall be stronger than the other people; and the elder shall serve the younger.* (Genesis 25:22-23)

The "younger" was Jacob and the "elder" Esau. Most are familiar with their story, but the familiarity should not deter us from understanding the clear providential hand of God in this story. It's interesting that the writer of Genesis devotes a full ten chapters to his life. He's clearly one of the unique characters in scripture in spite of the fact that much of his life is a study in what **not** to do in following God. Yet, follow God he did and God's plan was fulfilled. The second major promise made to Jacob is found in Genesis 28:12-15 in the famous "Jacob's Ladder" story.

> *And he dreamed, and behold a ladder set up on the earth, and the top of it reached to heaven: and behold the angels of God ascending and descending on it. And, behold, the LORD stood above it, and said, I am the LORD God of Abraham thy father, and the God of*

Isaac: the land whereon thou liest, to thee will I give it, and to thy seed; and thy seed shall be as the dust of the earth, and thou shalt spread abroad to the west, and to the east, and to the north, and to the south: and in thee and in thy seed shall all the families of the earth be blessed. And, behold, I am with thee, and will keep thee in all places whither thou goest, and will bring thee again into this land; for I will not leave thee, until I have done that which I have spoken to thee of.

This would be **Point A – Part Two**. There are some important things to remember here. Between these two wonderful promises concerning Jacob, there is the infamous selling of the birthright and the stealing of blessing. At this point Jacob is not exactly known for his honesty and integrity. In fact, he's living up to his name Jacob, "The Supplanter" or today we might simply call him "The Cheater." He clearly cheats his brother and blatantly deceives his own father. You could absolutely reach the conclusion that God simply cannot use someone like that; however, you would be terribly wrong.

Let's fast forward to the current day, thousands of years later. On almost any given day there will be news about a tiny little country in the Middle East. In fact, this tiny little country is the very center of all that happens in the Middle East. If you are a student of prophecy you are fully aware that this little dot on the world map is the center of God's plan for this entire planet. It's a country called Israel. Now where did that name come from? It's the "new" name given to Jacob by God. Yes, Israel and Jacob are the same person. Every time you see the name Israel you see an "in-your-face illustration" of the point I'm trying desperately to drive home. Here is a cheater deceiver from an in incredibly dysfunctional home and you can't open a newspaper thousands of years after his death without seeing his name. Think there might be hope for you? If you're beginning to see that, we're making progress! It's all about remembering Whose you are.

We need to stop for a minute and make something abundantly clear, however. Jacob is not a passive observer watching God work out His plan. *Far from it.* I hope you're not getting the idea that all you have to do is sit back and watch God plan out a wonderful path ahead for you. That was not Jacob's experience at all. It's important to remember that Jacob suffered some pretty stiff consequences for his rebellion and deception. But the point is that through it all Jacob had a desire to serve God. Did he always display it? *Far from it.* However, deep within him was a yearning for an intimate walk with his Creator and that's what God could see from the foundation of the world (Ephesians 1:4). God saw through the failure, the scheming, and the deception to a heart with a desire for fellowship with Him. That brings us to *Peniel,* the key experience between Jacob's Point A and Point B.

After deceiving his father and stealing his brother's blessing, Jacob is encouraged by his mother to run for his life. The threat of Esau killing him was probably not an idle threat. Jacob flees to his mother's homeland where the familiar story of Leah and Rachel unfolds. The deceiver is deceived by his father-in-law. For a time, the schemer is out schemed but he soon prospers and spends years in a weird competition with his wives' father and family. Remember the heart for God? After many years Jacob's heart yearns to make things right and go back home. Our loving God sees that heart and says, in Genesis 21:3, "And the LORD said unto Jacob, Return unto the land of thy fathers, and to thy kindred; and I will be with thee."

What you choose to believe will determine whether you ever make it to your Point B.

Well, that sounds good. Let's go home! There's just one problem, the mess Jacob had left behind. I think that keeps a lot of people from "going home" because they've left a mess or two of their own. For Jacob going home meant having to deal with his brother who wanted to kill him the last time they saw each other. Yet, he has the promise of God. Often we find the harsh circumstances of life coming into direct conflict with the promises of God. What you choose to believe will determine whether you ever make it to your Point B. That sounds simple enough but in reality it's not simple or easy at all. It certainly wasn't for Jacob. To be blunt, he was scared to death. Can you identify with Jacob?

What we have done and who we have been can become barriers to the image of Christ shining through us. Your past may be filled with walls that keep others from seeing Christ in you. In fact, when you look at your inner "image" mirror, you may see much more of your past than

His presence. Your regrets, failures, and patterns of blaming others could be hindering the promises of God about you and your future. So, will you allow past messes to contaminate present and future plans of God for you?

I remember extremely well when my wife and I made the choice to resign a very successful pastorate to begin CrossPower Ministries. We were finishing twenty-five years of ministry in a church we founded. We had struggled like every church, but we had finally begun to see God do everything that we had prayed for. Yet, God made it abundantly clear that our ministry was finished and that we were to step out in faith and trust Him for our needs. We knew we were following God's direction, but I must say there were times of pure fear as we stepped into the unknown. I wish I could be super pious and tell you that we just trusted God and never doubted for a moment God's provision. That would be a lie because there were passing moments of pure terror. But God knew our hearts and we knew His.

Jacob begins his journey home and the fulfillment of God's promise and plan for his life—His point B. It's a long journey and his nights on the road are filled with doubt and consternation about what he's going to face when he sees his brother, Esau. Genesis 32:7 sums it up, "Then Jacob was greatly afraid and distressed." Please remember that Jacob is still very much a work in progress. As he gets closer to home, he divides up his large family into two groups and he hides behind the women and children as they travel closer to Esau. What a guy! He was hiding behind his family.

Consider a moment the way we hide behind our families. Some of us hide behind the lack of family. Others hide behind their weaknesses, blaming them for the way we are. Still others use their accomplishments as our credentials for getting what we cannot achieve or earn. Yes, family can become our scapegoat or our only claim to being "somebody." We can blame them for the fear within us—fear of failure or success. Look at how Jacob hides behind family.

In Genesis 32:11 he prays, "Deliver me, I pray thee, from the hand of my brother, from the hand of Esau: for I fear him." Wow, talk about bravery! Remember, he's a work in progress. The night before he arrives back home, Jacob experiences the event that defined the rest of his life. It's the single most important event in Jacob's journey from Point A to Point B.

And Jacob was left alone; and there wrestled a man with him until the breaking of the day. And when he saw that he prevailed not against him, he touched the hollow of his thigh; and the hollow of Jacob's thigh was out of joint, as he wrestled with him. And he said, Let me go, for the day breaketh. And he said, I will not let thee go, except thou bless me. And he said unto him, What is thy name? And he said, Jacob. And he said, Thy name shall be called no more Jacob, but Israel: for as a prince hast thou power with God and with men, and hast prevailed. And Jacob asked him, and said, Tell me, I pray thee, thy name. And he said, Wherefore is it that thou dost ask after my name? And he blessed him there. And Jacob called the name of the place Peniel: for I have seen God face to face, and my life is preserved. And as he passed over Penuel the sun rose upon him, and he halted upon his thigh. (Genesis 32:24-31)

This certainly is one of the strangest events recorded in God's Word: a man "wrestling" with God. I'll let the academics debate all the fine theological points of this occurrence, but there are some things we can be certain of. Jacob had an encounter with God that changed his life forever. Jacob was in such desperate need for God's strength, protection, and blessing that he prays in the midst of the wrestling match, "I will not let thee go, except thou bless me." Is that presumptuous? *Not at all.* Here is a man who is about to face a situation that is above and beyond his strength, ability, and resources.

Please remember that it was God who put him here. It was God who told him to go home. Jacob knows that without God's supernatural presence he is doomed. Yes, without God's Presence we cannot and should not go any place, "And he said unto him, If thy presence go not with me, carry us not up hence" (Exodus 33:15). Where you are is where God has placed you; don't move until His Presence leads you. Until then, where He has you is not a bad place to be in. If you have not yet been in Jacob's situation, I can almost assure you that you will be. God often brings us to the very end of our strength and resources so that He can fill us with His strength and resources. Only when we are at the end of our rope and let go can we experience the net of His provision. Jacob is desperate and he refuses to let go of God. That's the New Testament principle of importunity at work in this story.

At this point something very strange occurs. God says, "What is thy name?" Now, why would God ask that? Did He have a momentary lapse of memory? Was God thinking, "I've got so many of you down there on earth I just can't keep track of you!" Was He about to say, "Hey, just give me the first letter and I'll remember." Of course not. The asking of Jacob's name was not for God's sake, it was for Jacob. Remember, his name meant something. God was not only asking, "Who are you?" He was also asking, "What are you?" I'm certain that Jacob knew exactly what was happening.

Before he responded, Jacob must have felt an overwhelming sense of shame as he rehearsed in his mind his recent orders to put all the women and children out front and the fright and fear deep within his breast about his upcoming encounter with his brother. He might have even remembered the events that started this whole chapter in his life when he was so deceptive with his father and brother. With thoughts of failure and fear racing through his mind, he bowed his head and answered God's question. "My name is Jacob." Possibly for the very first time he understood what his name really meant and that he had become the fulfillment of all its negative connotations. In essence he was saying to God, "I'm the deceiver, the supplanter, the schemer. That is who I am and what I am." It was a painful but transforming admission. It was exactly what God had been waiting for!

Scripture promises that if we confess our sins, God is faithful and just to forgive us (1 John 1:9). To confess means "to say the same as, to agree with." Jacob was agreeing with God about who he had been. None of us can change who and what we are without first agreeing with God about what a mess we have been and have created. We look back and confess. We look now and confess. We look forward to forgiveness and becoming a new creation in Christ. This transformation process is seen in Jacob.

Instantly, without hesitation, God responds with the incredible pronouncement, "Thy name shall be called no more Jacob, but Israel: for as a prince hast thou power with God and with men, and has prevailed." Jacob was suddenly well on his way to his Point B. God had been patiently waiting for Jacob to admit who and what he was. For years, Jacob had been trying to fake it and make it in his own strength. He was asking for God to help him, but did not want God to have him. That's a huge difference! When Jacob finally came to the absolute bottom, the pit, the end, and admitted what he was without God at the very center of his life, God was ready and willing to change Jacob from the inside out and make him the man of God he needed to be.

You'll notice that Jacob came out of this wrestling match with a decided limp. His thigh was put out of joint. I'm told that the hip joint is the strongest joint in the body. Shoulders go out of joint, elbows, and fingers go out of joint, but never a hip. God wanted to make it clear to Jacob that his strength was no match for God's, and He left him with that limp as a constant reminder.

I have come to love this story because it is my story. Whenever I do anything in my strength, my wisdom, and my power I fail miserably. Time and again God has allowed or caused situations in my life, family, and ministry to remind me of the power of my own flesh.

I clearly remember a meeting I was having with my Board of Deacons many years ago. I was a very young pastor in my first pastorate and had just attended a pastor's conference at a Christian College where some of the "biggies" were telling the rest of us how to be a successful leader. In one of the sessions on "leadership" one of the well-known Christian leaders told us that in order to be a real leader one must always provide a solution to the problem at hand. He went on to imply that even if your solution is deficient—as a leader you must present it to prove that you're in charge. Well, this meeting with the deacons was my first opportunity to put in practice what I had heard from the expert. I don't even remember now what the presenting problem was, but when it came up I didn't have a clue what to do or what to suggest as an answer. I felt a moment of terrible panic. I was the pastor, the leader and I had no clue what the answer was!

I broke into a sweat for a few minutes and then suddenly blurted out a "solution." In hindsight, it was a really dumb suggestion and it didn't even take hindsight for my deacons to quickly realize my solution was totally unfeasible for the situation at hand. Well, my board members began to quickly and, praise God, kindly pick apart my argument. But, *I was the leader!* I thought this was a challenge to my leadership so I determined that it was now my responsibility to prove who was in charge. It was not pretty; by God's grace, I had some mature men who realized that their young, immature pastor felt threatened and simply allowed me to make a complete fool of myself. You've heard the old saying about giving someone enough rope to hang themselves. Well, I had an abundant amount of rope! As I look back, it was nothing but my pride and accepting some very bad advice as Gospel. I wish that was the last time my pride got me into trouble! Yes, I get the whole Jacob thing. *I am Jacob!* Sadly, at times he has been my patron saint.

How long have you been faking it in your own strength? How many times have you found yourself trying to scheme your way out of another mess that has consumed you because you did it your way instead of God's? Is it possible that as you read these words the Holy Spirit of God is asking you, "What is your name?" You've tried to make deals with God. You've made all kinds of wonderful promises. You may have even "rededicated" your life. You may have been to an altar repeatedly and poured out your heart with assurances to God that you will "do better." Is it possible that God is just waiting for you to admit that without Him you're a total failure and that you have been doing everything your way instead of His? He wants to transform you. He wants to conform you to the image of His Son, but it must be His work accomplished through your surrender. You do belong to Him. He has every right to full control. You've been purchased by His blood. He wants you to remember Whose You Are.

Jacob did become the great Father of Israel. That precious nation still bears his name as a constant reminder of what God can do with an individual that comes to full and complete surrender. Jacob was broken in the process; in fact brokenness was the process. Now, whenever you hear anything about Israel in the news you can be reminded of the process of getting from Point A to Point B **and remember Whose you are.**

Reflect and Apply

Take a moment and reflect on what you just read. Be "Judgment Seat Honest" as you answer these questions.

? *At times has it been difficult to see God's plan for your life?*
? *Are you yearning for an intimate walk with your Creator?*
? *Can you identify with Jacob?*
? *Have you been trying to fake it and make it on your own strength?*

? *Have you been asking God to help you when in reality, He needs to have you?*

? *How many times have you found yourself trying to scheme your way out of another mess that has consumed you because you did it your way instead of God's?*

? *Is it possible that the Holy Spirit of God is asking you, "What is your name?"*

? *Have you hidden behind family issues of the past and blamed them on your failure?*

Chapter Seven

BIBLICAL EXAMPLES OF GOD'S PROVIDENCE–JOSEPH AND MOSES

Joseph

And Joseph dreamed a dream, and he told it his brethren: and they hated him yet the more. And he said unto them, Hear, I pray you, this dream which I have dreamed: For, behold, we were binding sheaves in the field, and, lo, my sheaf arose, and also stood upright; and, behold, your sheaves stood round about, and made obeisance to my sheaf. And his brethren said to him, Shalt thou indeed reign over us? or shalt thou indeed have dominion over us? And they hated him yet the more for his dreams, and for his words. And he dreamed yet another dream, and told it his brethren, and said, Behold, I have dreamed a dream more; and, behold, the sun and the moon and the eleven stars made obeisance to me. And he told it to his father, and to his brethren: and his father rebuked him, and said unto him, What is this dream that thou hast dreamed? Shall I and thy mother and thy brethren indeed come to bow down ourselves to thee to the earth? And his brethren envied him; but his father observed the saying. (Genesis 37:5-11)

Did you ever dream that you were someone famous? I suppose most people have dreamed that they were their favorite sports hero, movie star, singer or entertainer. I confess, I'm totally weird and I have witnesses to prove it! I have dreamed that I was one famous preacher or another. I have dreamed several times that I was C.H. Spurgeon, that great preacher of the mid-eighteenth century England. I always hoped my dreams were wrought because of honor and not envy. Joseph, the larger than life character of the Old Testament, had some dreams as well, but his dreams were straight from God. Those dreams became Joseph's Point A and revealed his Point B.

Family issues often are obstacles in our journey to being what God wants us to be.

Joseph was the favorite son of Jacob. This caused a great deal of jealousy and anger from his brothers even before the two dreams in our text above. The dreams, although from God, did nothing to help. In fact, as the Word clearly tells us, Joseph's dreams caused the hatred from the brothers to deepen. Family issues often are obstacles in our journey to being what God wants us to be and that was certainly the case with Joseph. We all desire a family that will support us and encourage us in our spiritual walk, but often that is simply not the case. Don't be fooled that this is an insurmountable obstacle as we will learn from this great man's life.

The dreams of Joseph began his journey to a very special work that God had prepared for him. The dreams marked Point A and the fulfillment of the dreams would be Point B. As usual there was a whole lot of "stuff" in between.

Joseph must have been filled with excitement and anticipation when he awoke from these two incredible dreams. It seems that somehow he knew they were God and not just too much late night pizza. Maybe in his day it would have been spicy hummus. Anyway, he knew they were filled with special meaning about his future. I'm certain he knew how his brothers felt about him, and these dreams must have indicated to him that one day all that animosity would be gone and they would respect him.

Those positive feelings didn't last long. His father sends him one day to check on his brothers who were tending the family flock of sheep. Joseph probably didn't relish the thought of spending time with family members who despised him, but he was an obedient son and did exactly what his father told him. Joseph is about to confront several incredibly difficult years and circumstances. It is extremely important to remember that many tests are to perfect, not correct.

It is extremely important to remember that many tests are to perfect, not correct.

Let me help you understand the process. Tests reveal both our strengths and our weaknesses. God disciplines us in our weaknesses; He doesn't punish. Discipline corrects and teaches; it's not for punishing and crushing us. As we grow and mature in Christ, we then go through tests that we have failed in the past and can now pass them. We have learned the answers and can be perfect in our answers—our Christ-like actions, feelings, and thoughts. Discipline corrects and teaches so that we can pass future tests and give glory to God for His perfecting work in us.

In the forward to this book, I shared that it was a severe test, a trial that spawned the beginning of the work you now hold in your hands. I'll never forget the specialist telling me that there was the possibility that I would never be able to speak again. What? But I was called to preach before I was a teenager! It was God who gave me a voice and I have tried to use it for Him my entire life. How could He possibly take it away from me? How could this possibly bring glory to Him? My voice is my instrument, my tool just as much as a musician or a mechanic. It's what I "do." Well, I assure you that you would not be reading these words were it not for that time of trial. It was just an interlude between my Point A and B.

So, remember that Joseph's brothers' hatred for him had reached a boiling point. When they saw him coming the plotting immediately began. Some want to kill him but one of his brothers had at least a small amount of pity for him and pleaded for his life. He's thrown into a pit while they figure out what to do with him. That must have been an interesting conversation. I might check out that DVD when I get to Heaven. As the negotiations over what to do with their brother continued, a band of slave traders happened to pass by.

With a little persuasion Judah, one of the brothers, convinced the others that if they killed him they would be rid of him, but here was an opportunity to get rid of the little jerk and make some money at the same time. The money evidently persuaded the others. Joseph was sold, his famous "coat of many colors" was retrieved, and Joseph was on his way to a life of denigration and servitude. The brothers went back home, told Dad that his favorite child had been eaten by some wild animals, and thought their problems were over. The brothers, however, did not bargain for the severe grief of their father or the sovereignty of God.

We'll hit the fast forward button at this point and fly through some of the immediate details while acknowledging God's constant hand on the circumstances. Joseph is sold by the traders but not to just anyone. He is sold to a very influential Egyptian by the name of Potiphar. Joseph is determined to honor God no matter what his circumstances, and he is immediately recognized by his new owner as a young man of exceptional ability. He's quickly promoted to a position of importance in the household. Yes, God was at work.

God often has interesting ways of getting us from Point A to Point B.

Joseph must also have been a pretty handsome man as Potiphar's wife noticed and made a totally non-subtle pass at him. Joseph, being a man of integrity, refused the advance and actually ran from the temptation. Obviously God rewarded his integrity with another promotion, right? Having been scorned, his boss's wife accused him of making a sexual advance towards her; exactly the opposite of what really happened. As a result, Joseph was arrested and thrown into prison.

As Joseph languished in a dark, damp dungeon he must have thought, "Where was this in those dreams?" Oh yes, God often has interesting ways of getting us from Point A to Point B. Between the two and unable to see either the promise or the fulfillment, we are tempted to doubt that God is in control at all.

There, of course, is the part of Joseph's story about the Pharaoh's butler and baker and their dreams, but we're on fast forward here. Just note that dreams are a big part of Joseph's life. Joseph was seemingly forgotten in prison and the dreams of his youth must have faded into oblivion. Or did they? We're not told much about Joseph's time in prison except that he was a model prisoner because he was determined to honor his God no matter what the circumstances. That brings us back to the subject of dreams, but this time it was Pharaoh's dreams. The Egyptian Pharaoh had two dreams that scared the scarabs right out of Pharaoh's crown. His magicians, sorcerers, and wise men were called and commanded to interpret the dreams. None of them had a clue and Pharaoh was not a happy camper. Finally, the butler who was supposed to put in a good word for Joseph, told the monarch that there's a guy in prison who was awesome at interpreting dreams. Joseph was called, interpreted the dreams, suddenly found himself the number two man in all of Egypt, and in charge of preparing for the terrible drought predicted in the dreams. You could get whiplash from that turn around in Joseph's condition and position.

When God is in control, it takes nothing for Him to change things.

The predicted famine came to pass and impacted this entire portion of the globe including Joseph's homeland. Like everyone else, Joseph's family needed food and there was only one place and one person they could obtain it. The brothers were sent by their father to Egypt to buy food, but they were totally unaware of what happened to the brother that they sold into slavery. They had no idea that they were facing their long lost brother and that he had their entire future in their hands. Because of his exalted position, when they were led into his presence they immediately knelt before him, just like the dreams!

The rest of the story is wonderful and significant. Joseph gets a little revenge, their father almost has a heart attack, and the entire family is saved by submitting to Joseph, just like the dreams. God had brought Joseph from A to B just like He said. There was a pit, deception, slavery, more deception, false accusations, prison, abandonment, and a whole lot more in between, but God was never out of control. When Joseph was going through the fire, God had His hand on the thermostat. Through it all Joseph maintained his faith in His God. He knew he belonged to God and that God would somehow, some way fulfill His plan for Joseph's life. Joseph stayed surrendered and God stayed in control.

I can't promise you that God will reveal His perfect plan for you in dreams. Scripture doesn't promise that. It does, however, promise that

God is in control and that "all things" really do work together for good while He is conforming us to the image of Christ. You're His child and His possession so **remember Whose you are.**

Moses

> *And Moses was learned in all the wisdom of the Egyptians, and was mighty in words and in deeds. And when he was full forty years old, it came into his heart to visit his brethren the children of Israel. And seeing one of them suffer wrong, he defended him, and avenged him that was oppressed, and smote the Egyptian: For he supposed his brethren would have understood how that God by his hand would deliver them: but they understood not.* (Acts 7:22-25)

We often hear of "late starters" like Harlan Sanders, who started selling his famous "secret recipe" chicken when he was sixty-five. However, reading the story of Moses starting a "career" at eighty reveals God's providence in a most amazing way. He was born a Hebrew during a time when the Pharaoh was determined to keep his kingdom safe from the rapidly growing descendants of Jacob by having all Hebrew male babies killed. Moses was spared by his mother, and through God's unique providence, was raised in the home of Pharaoh by his daughter. You have to love God's sense of humor.

When God has a plan—no man will stop it.

Moses was raised in the lap of Egyptian luxury with the finest in material possessions and education. We're not certain when he realized that he was a Hebrew and we're not completely certain as to when he realized that God had called him to a very special job as the deliverer of God's people from Egypt after 450 years of slavery. The account of his "calling" is very vague in the book of Exodus and strangely we learn more in the New Testament book of Acts.

From the Exodus narrative we learn about Moses visiting his "brethren" and the killing of the Egyptian oppressor, but it is not until the book of Acts was written that we learn Moses was forty years old and most importantly, that Moses knew that he had been called by God to be the deliverer of the children of Israel. This is Point A for Moses. Point B would be the fulfillment of that task. Easy, right?

Evidently, Moses felt a deep compulsion to do something about the plight of his brethren, but he didn't wait for God's instructions. He developed his own plan. Can you say, "Epic failure?" He goes down to scope out the situation and is confronted with the terrible conditions the Hebrews had been enduring for generations. He is overcome with "duty" and decides to start the "deliverance" immediately. Obviously, his plan was not very well thought out and possibly it was just a result of emotion. Whatever the case it was clearly not the way God had planned for the deliverance to take place. Moses had taken things into his own hands and it did not go well. Can you identify? I certainly can.

The story is very familiar so let's just look at the summary of how God brought Moses from Point A to Point B. Moses has to flee Egypt for his life. From a human stand point Moses was a total failure. God had spent forty years preparing Moses for this special mission. He had spared him from a wicked Pharaoh, given him the best education on the planet, and provided access to the only human capable of setting the Hebrews free. Moses destroyed the whole plan in one afternoon; or so it seemed. When we fail the enemy of our soul loves to convince us that we're done, finished. He wickedly rehearses our failure over and over again in our hearts. He fiendishly reminds us of our weakness and ineptitude. He tempts us to act contrary to God's plan and then throws our failure in our face. His strategy has never changed. No wonder he is referred to as the "accuser of the brethren" in Revelation 12:10.

Moses found himself somewhere out on the backside of a lonely desert leading not a nation of people but a herd of dumb sheep. I can only imagine some of the conversations Moses must have had with himself while tending to lambs and sheep. "Why was I so proud? Why did I get ahead of God? Why didn't I do things God's way? I'll never fulfill the purpose of God in my life! I blew it! I'm finished!" The bleating of the sheep must have seemed like a congregation shouting amen as he beat himself up for another forty years.

While there certainly are consequences for our actions and failures, our God has this miraculous ability to take us from Point A to Point B in the most unusual ways.

Moses is put on the spiritual shelf for forty years. What a long, painful interlude between Point A and Point B. For Moses the intermission was not just long, he thought it was permanent. Do you feel that your past failure has permanently disqualified you from God's service? While there certainly are consequences for our actions and failures, our God has this miraculous ability to take us from Point A to Point B in the most unusual ways.

After forty years of sheep time, Moses is confronted with the spectacular bush that burned but was not consumed. It was there that God made it clear that He had not forgotten the promise made to Moses many years before. Something happened to Moses during his years at Wooly University. Forty years earlier, Moses rushed to serve God in his own strength. He didn't wait for God's full instruction and he certainly did not depend on God's power. This time is totally different. The once proud, Egyptian educated, self-sufficient Moses is now humble and dependent.

Now Moses kept the flock of Jethro his father in law, the priest of Midian: and he led the flock to the backside of the desert, and came to the mountain of God, even to Horeb. And the angel of the LORD appeared unto him in a flame of fire out of the midst of a bush: and he looked, and, behold, the bush burned with fire, and the bush was not consumed. And Moses said, I will now turn aside, and see this great sight, why the bush is not burnt. And when the LORD saw that he turned aside to see, God called unto him out of the midst of the bush, and said, Moses, Moses. And he said, Here am I. And he said, Draw not nigh hither: put off thy shoes from off thy feet, for the place whereon thou standest is holy ground. Moreover he said, I am the God of thy father, the God of Abraham, the God of Isaac, and the God of Jacob. And Moses hid his face; for he was afraid to look upon God. And the LORD said, I have surely seen the affliction of my people which are in Egypt, and have heard their cry by reason of their taskmasters; for I know their sorrows; And I am come down to deliver them out of the hand of the Egyptians, and to bring them up out of that land unto a good land and a large, unto a land flowing with milk and honey; unto the place of the Canaanites, and the Hittites, and the Amorites, and the Perizzites, and the Hivites, and the Jebusites. Now therefore, behold, the cry of the children of Israel is come unto me: and I have also seen the oppression wherewith the Egyptians oppress them. Come now therefore, and I will send thee unto Pharaoh, that thou mayest bring forth my people the children of Israel out of Egypt. And Moses said unto God, Who am I, that I should go unto Pharaoh, and that I should bring forth the children of Israel out of Egypt? And he said, Certainly I will be with thee; and this shall be a token unto thee, that I have sent thee: When thou hast brought forth the people out of Egypt, ye shall serve God upon this mountain. And Moses said unto God, Behold, when I come unto the children of Israel, and shall say unto them, The God of your fathers hath sent me unto you; and they shall say to me, What is his name? what shall I say unto them? And God said unto Moses, I AM THAT I AM: and he said, Thus shalt thou say unto the children of Israel, I AM hath sent me unto you. (Exodus 3:1-14)

What a change! This is a different man! God speaks to him out of this burning bush and reveals the rest of the plan that had originally been given to Moses forty years earlier. God's purpose in choosing Moses is unmistakable. I mean, how often do you see a burning bush in the middle of the desert? This doesn't mean get the s'mores; it means listen up! Instead of responding with, "Yes, God! You've got the right man! Just give me the plan and I'll kiss the little wool balls goodbye!" Moses' first response is, "Who am I?" This time around he needs to be convinced. After all, he's a big time loser and he's an old dude now—he's eighty years old! He blew his chance years ago. What Moses did not understand was he had not yet arrived at his Point B and God was determined to get him there and use "all things" to do it.

The question is never about God's faithfulness, it is always about our surrender which often comes through experiences of failure, defeat, weakness, and almost always brokenness.

Moses did lead the children of Israel out of Egyptian bondage and through the wilderness and make it to Point B. It was not easy even with the miraculous power of God on his side. The journey from A to B is never easy, but God is bringing things into your life to accomplish exactly that. He's using all things to make you more like Jesus. You are sealed in providence. The question is never about God's faithfulness, it is always about our surrender. That surrender often comes through experiences of failure, defeat, weakness, and almost always brokenness.

I'm hesitant to share something very intimate and personal because when you realize what a failure prone author you are reading—you might just lay this book aside. However, I'll take the risk and trust God. My wife and I have an absolutely phenomenal marriage. As I write these words, we have been married forty-four years and we are deeply in love. Sadly, our marriage was not always so wonderful. We went through several years that we refer to as the "seven years of Hell" and we're not trying to be facetious. It was truly a time of Hell. We were facing some serious issues with our children and it seemed like my wife and I could agree on nothing. My pride grew to brand new heights as we faced these struggles. I was trying to publicly pastor a growing church while privately dealing with deeply serious marital and family problems. I worked very hard at putting on a good "front" before the congregation, but my home was completely falling apart. We became about as dysfunctional as a family could be, but somehow I wore the pastor mask at church and very few people knew what was going on within the walls of our house. I was a complete and total phony. My ministry was a charade.

Well, I'm pretty good at playing games but my wife is not. She finally had enough of my duplicity and called some of the leaders of the church and simply told them the truth about their pastor. I received one of those calls that every pastor dreads. "Hello, pastor. The Board is here at the church and we would like for you to join us as quickly as you can get here." When I arrived at this surprise meeting—there was my wife and all my men. The chairman of the church board informed me that my wife had informed them that I was one person at church and completely different at home. Inside, I was furious! I'm not sure I've ever been so angry.

Outwardly I was calm and cool—for a short time. After a brief time, it was pretty clear to all that my wife was far more truthful than I was. The men expressed their deep love for me, my wife and our family, but they also made it clear that something had to be done and quickly. I won't bore you with details, but I was "removed" from the pulpit and was forced to take a three month sabbatical. The church was willing to pay for a counselor, continue my pay, and support me in any way possible, but I had to get my home in order before I could return to the pulpit. I've never been so humiliated in my life. It was my pride that had gotten me to this place and that gigantic pride was brought suddenly down to the pits. Again, I won't go into all the details but we did seek counseling, we honestly dealt with the issue that had gotten us to the crisis, and God brought about incredible healing and restoration. Our marriage was saved and now thrives beyond anything we could have imagined.

Now, what about the church? Because of my pride, one of my greatest fears was that because of all this my ministry would be over and I would be forever disqualified from preaching and pastoring. I was called to preach when I was twelve years old and I have known from that time that preaching was what God wanted me to do. I was certain that was all over. Again, God's grace....

Yes, I did return to the pulpit where a wonderful grace-filled church welcomed me back with love and acceptance. In fact, the greatest years of ministry in that church occurred after those events. God had tested and disciplined and He alone deserves the glory. Also, those seven years of Hell have become the foundation for much of what my wife and I teach in our Marriage Conferences. They have given us unique insight into the struggles that many couples face in their own marriages. We continually hear, "Finally, someone understands what we're going through" – and we can look them in the eye and assure them that yes, we do understand. Instead of that trial, testing, and disciplining disqualifying me from ministry it has become the foundation for future ministry. But I had to become totally broken before the Lord before He could do the work in me that He desired. God loves a broken heart. Although the breaking process is often incredibly painful, it is always beneficial, and if we come to complete surrender He will always heal and restore.

Here's a closing lesson to learn from the life of Moses. When God had finished the "learning and breaking" experience of the desert, Moses could not believe that he could still be used by God. He responds to the call of God with, "Who AM I?" God responds with "I AM." It's not who you are – it's **Whose you are!**

Reflect and Apply

? *Do family issues feel like they are obstacles in your journey to being what God wants us to be?*

? *Have you been fooled into thinking this is an insurmountable obstacle?*

? *What did you learn from the life of Joseph about this?*

? *How did learning that many testings are to perfect, not correct change your perception of these testings?*

? *What interesting ways has God used to get you from Point A to Point B?*

? *Have you ever been overcome with "duty" and tried to start the "deliverance" without obtaining God's full instructions?*

? *Has the enemy tried to remind you of your weakness and ineptitude?*

? *Have you felt that your past failure has permanently disqualified you from God's service?*

? *How has this concept changed as a result of studying the life of Moses?*

? *Have you ever thought that God's attempt to bring you to Brokenness was meant to destroy you? How did you move beyond that thought?*

? *What do you understand to be the difference between Brokenness and Desperation?*

Chapter Eight

BIBLICAL EXAMPLES OF GOD'S PROVIDENCE – DAVID

D avid is completely unique among all the characters of scripture. In spite of all the godly men and women revealed to us on the pages of the Bible, no one else is called "a man after God's own heart" (Acts 13:22), and no one else was more unlikely or unworthy.

David's Point A is found in 1 Samuel 16 and it's also where we find the first mention of his Point B. As we enter the chapter we intersect the downward plunge of Saul, the first king of Israel. He had been anointed to be king by Samuel the prophet, but had deliberately disobeyed God and been rejected from being king. It was time for Samuel to anoint a new man as the leader of God's people.

> *Now the LORD said to Samuel, "How long will you mourn for Saul, seeing I have rejected him from reigning over Israel? Fill your horn with oil, and go; I am sending you to Jesse the Bethlehemite. For I have provided myself a king among his sons."* (1 Samuel 16:1)

Samuel immediately obeys God and heads to Jesse's house. Can you imagine the excitement of this father! He has a knock on his door and suddenly he is face to face with the famous prophet, Samuel telling him that one of his sons will be the next king! Pretty sweet for a Dad! Jesse lines up the boys in order of age although he doesn't think it's even necessary to bring in all the sons because, certainly, the oldest boy named Eliab would be Samuel's choice. As his oldest stands before Samuel Jesse proudly pronounces, "Surely the Lord's anointed is before him" (1 Samuel 16:6). Samuel takes a look and God says, "No." No problem! Number two son is brought before the prophet. Nope. Number three – ditto.

So, seven sons are paraded before Samuel with the same response, "No, not this one," until seven sons have been rejected and no one else is in the house. Everyone is confused, especially the Prophet of God. He was certain he got the instructions correct from God to go to Jesse's house and anoint one of his sons to be the next king. In total frustration Samuel asked Jesse if he has any other sons. The response is shocking. Yes, he has one more son but, well, he's a nice kid, in fact a cute kid, but he was not exactly king material. Jesse didn't even consider bringing son number eight before Samuel. Here's where it really gets weird. David's father has to be threatened in order for him to bring in the last son to see the prophet.

> *And Samuel said to Jesse, "Are all the young men here?" Then he said, "There remains yet the youngest, and there he is, keeping the sheep." And Samuel said to Jesse, "Send and bring him. For we will not sit down till he comes here."* (1 Samuel 16:11)

Samuel tells Jesse that he's not leaving and he's not even going to sit down until the last son is brought from the sheep fields. Talk about an unlikely king! His own father saw no potential in him whatsoever to be the next leader of God's people. There must have been an incredible hush in that the room when David entered. All eyes were on the young sheep herder as he stood before the mighty prophet of God. The hush was exchanged for gasps as Samuel says, "The Lord said, 'Arise, anoint him: for this is he'" (I Samuel 16:12). David, are you kidding me? Yes, David, possibly the most unlikely person in the kingdom was chosen by God as the next monarch. Point A was his "anointing" and the promise of Point B was his "coronation." Sounds easy, doesn't it? David is chosen by God Himself out of everyone else in the kingdom, so he just has to wait for the coronation, right?

The life of David is a literal roller coaster flying from fantastic mountain top to deep, dark valley. Many of David's greatest psalms were written in the dark valleys where it seems at times he was approaching despair and despondency before he was suddenly rushing to another triumphal mountain experience. His choice by Samuel was certainly one of the highest mountain tops. A young kid, rejected by his family is chosen to be king of God's chosen people.

We're not certain about the amount of time between Point A and Point B but we are certain of the events. There is, of course, the whole Goliath thing which is one of the most familiar stories in the entire Bible. Little David is the only one willing to take on the giant, Goliath. Standing at almost nine feet tall he must have been an imposing figure, especially with his massive armor shining in the sun. David chose five smooth stones from a creek, but he needed only one to bring the mighty behemoth to the ground and then off with his head. This experience suddenly catapulted David to fame although most, at this time, had no clue that he had been anointed to be the next king as Saul demonstrates that he is not going to give up the throne easily.

The timing is a little difficult and controversial, but we know that David became a part of the inner circle of Saul's household and court. He becomes a mighty warrior which, strangely, led to some of the most difficult days in the pilgrimage from Point A to Point B.

So David went out wherever Saul sent him, and behaved wisely. And Saul set him over the men of war, and he was accepted in the sight of all the people and also in the sight of Saul's servants. Now it had happened as they were coming home, when David was returning from the slaughter of the Philistine, that the women had come out of all the cities of Israel, singing and dancing, to meet King Saul, with tambourines, with joy, and with musical instruments. So the women sang as they danced, and said: "Saul has slain his thousands, and David his ten thousands." Then Saul was very angry, and the saying displeased him; and he said, "They have ascribed to David ten thousands, and to me they have ascribed only thousands. Now what more can he have but the kingdom?" So Saul eyed David from that day forward. (1 Samuel 18:5-9)

Saul kept a close and very jealous eye on David from then on. This begins the "cat and mouse" relationship between David the next king of Israel and Saul the current, mentally ill and flesh-filled king. David is desperate to remain loyal to King Saul, but it's almost impossible considering Saul's mental condition, and his determination to keep David from reaching his throne. These are brutal years for David as he is continually running from cave to cave and forest to forest trying to save his life while staying true to his God. He is successful in saving his life, but at times fails miserably at being faithful to God. He sinks so deep into depression that at one point he pretends to be insane and flees to the enemy.

> *And David arose and fled that day for fear of Saul, and went to Achish the king of Gath. And the servants of Achish said unto him, Is not this David the king of the land? did they not sing one to another of him in dances, saying, Saul hath slain his thousands, and David his ten thousands? And David laid up these words in his heart, and was sore afraid of Achish the king of Gath. And he changed his behaviour before them, and feigned himself mad in their hands, and scrabbled on the doors of the gate, and let his spittle fall down upon his beard. Then said Achish unto his servants, Lo, ye see the man is mad: wherefore then have ye brought him to me? Have I need of mad men, that ye have brought this fellow to play the mad man in my presence? Shall this fellow come into my house?*
> (1 Samuel 21:10-15)

What a sad spectacle. Did you notice where this took place? Gath. Recognize that name? Yes, that's the home town of Goliath. If any place should have reminded David of God's hand upon him it should have been here. To add to the sad irony, if you look at the context, David is actually holding in his hand the sword of Goliath that David had used to cut off the giant's head! Not only does David retreat to the arch enemies of God and His people, he makes a complete fool of himself. To add to this disgraceful period, David is also responsible for the death of eighty-five priests.

Years pass as the contest between Saul and David continues. David must have spent many nights gazing up into the heavens asking God about that day so long ago when Samuel had poured the oil on his head and announced that he was to be king. It was now only a faint, painful memory. *King? He's lucky to be alive,* he thought. *King? Never.* All of the circumstances screamed in David's face, telling him he would never reach his Point B.

It's very possible that you are in a similar situation. You may not have someone trying to kill you, but I'm certain you have some giants staring at you and you may feel like God has abandoned you. Well, as they say, stay tuned. David's story is not over, not by a long shot! It does get worse, however, **for a time**.

Things often become worse as God accomplishes His plan for us and those we love. Sometimes God chooses to go to extraordinary measures to accomplish that plan. One of the most incredible experiences of my life occurred during those "seven years of Hell" that I talked about in the last chapter. Our family was in terrible shape and in the midst of our despair we were trying to love and discipline our prodigal. Our son is one of the finest young men you will ever meet and God has blessed him with a wonderful family, but he went through some extremely rough years. He had run away on a few occasions and each time our parental hearts broke in two. When we would discover his absence my wife would call everyone she could think of to pray for our precious son. If it was an extended period of time, she would call all the hospitals in our area as well as the police "just in case."

On one particular evening he had left again—this time leaving us a very disturbing note. Panic set in as we were consumed with fear for his safety. My wife mentioned that she would begin calling our prayer warriors and enlist their prayers as well as the hospitals and police. She was desperate to find her son as was I, but this time I had a strange sense from the Lord that this time was to be different. I told her that I felt very strongly that we should tell no one but God. No one. It was a very long night and we cried out to God for the safety of our son. We would pray, cry, and try futilely to sleep. Sometime around 5:30 a.m. the next morning, our phone rang. It was the Highway Patrol and they had picked up our son hitchhiking on an interstate highway north of our home. It was one of the most wonderful phone calls we had ever received. He was safe!

The officer told us that our son didn't want to come to us—that he preferred to be taken to a friend's house. At that point all I cared about was that he was safe, so I told them that he could be taken to the friend's house and I would pick him up later that day. We praised

God for answered prayer and tried to catch a little sleep as the new day began. Later in the day I drove to the friend's house to bring our son home. I was thrilled to see him but he was clearly not happy to see me. He got into the car and immediately said, "Why do you worry so much! I would have been fine! Why did you call everyone and tell them I was gone?"

I told him that we had told no one but God; we had chosen to do nothing but pray. He clearly did not believe me and I inquired why. He told me that he was walking up the interstate when a Highway Patrolman drove up beside him and rolled down the passenger window. At that point, the officer said, "Is your name Tim?"

When he replied in the affirmative the officer continued and said, "Get in, son – I've been looking for you all night." My jaw dropped when I heard this and assured my son that we had told no one, absolutely no one. The reply was, "Then, how did he know my name!" I had no answer and at that point he wouldn't have believed anything I said anyway. When I told my wife of this miraculous circumstance, we both collapsed to the floor in praise. To this day I have no idea who that officer was and how he knew our son's name. Was he an angel? Had God somehow supernaturally informed him of our son? We don't know. All we know is that we dedicated our son to God when He was a baby, and God wonderfully protected him through some incredibly difficult teenage years. It was many years later before our son finally believed what really transpired that incredible evening. He was clearly sealed in God's providence.

That was a time of our desperation and God's provision; now back to David. David's desperation grows and deepens. As incredible as it may seem, this "man after God's heart" comes to such darkness that he decides to just give up and sell out to the enemy.

> *And David said in his heart, "Now I shall perish someday by the hand of Saul. There is nothing better for me than that I should speedily escape to the land of the Philistines; and Saul will despair of me, to seek me anymore in any part of Israel. So I shall escape out of his hand." Then David arose and went over with the six hundred men who were with him to Achish the son of Maoch, king of Gath. So David dwelt with Achish at Gath, he and his men, each man*

with his household, and David with his two wives, Ahinoam the Jezreelitess, and Abigail the Carmelitess, Nabal's widow. And it was told Saul that David had fled to Gath; so he sought him no more. Then David said to Achish, "If I have now found favor in your eyes, let them give me a place in some town in the country, that I may dwell there. For why should your servant dwell in the royal city with you?" So Achish gave him Ziklag that day. Therefore Ziklag has belonged to the kings of Judah to this day. Now the time that David dwelt in the country of the Philistines was one full year and four months. (1 Samuel 27:1-7)

Yes, David is back at Gath but not as a maniac this time, but rather a traitor. The Philistines are the arch enemies of God and here is the next king of Israel swearing loyalty to their enemies. The account is sickening! David says that he is "your servant" to Achish the pagan king. Surely David will see his error and repent! But in fact, it seems that this total capitulation to the enemy works out great! David is given his own little city for his family and his rag tag "army" of men, and Saul **stopped** pursuing him. He's free from Saul! But he's a total sell out. Stop the presses!

Let's chase an important rabbit for just a minute. David is clearly sinning and rebelling against God and it looks like it's actually working out. David was clearly deceived at this point by the enemy of our soul. He convinced David that serving God was just too tough. Stop trying to honor God, it just isn't worth it. David took it in hook, line, and sinker. He had forgotten that a hook makes you a captive. Sin looks wonderful and liberating for a time. But that false freedom never lasts and always ends in true bondage. Don't take the bait!

An Old time Tent preacher is quoted as saying, "Sin will take you farther than you want to go, keep you longer than you want to stay, and cost you more than you want to pay."

The famous preacher, R.G. Lee once said, "The Devil always pays in counterfeit bills." This was certainly true of David. His security and "freedom" was short lived. It appears David will never get to Point B. Hang tight—it ain't over yet. God's grace and mercy are incredible things. How in the world does God straighten out this mess? His next king is hanging out and chilling with the enemy. I love God's sense of humor and His divine determination to fulfill His plan in our lives. David's journey from A to B takes a decidedly weird turn.

Now the Philistines gathered together all their armies to Aphek: and the Israelites pitched by a fountain which is in Jezreel. And the lords of the Philistines passed on by hundreds, and by thousands: but David and his men passed on in the rereward with Achish. Then said the princes of the Philistines, What do these Hebrews here? And Achish said unto the princes of the Philistines, Is not this David, the servant of Saul the king of Israel, which hath been with me these days, or these years, and I have found no fault in him since he fell unto me unto this day? And the princes of the Philistines were wroth with him; and the princes of the Philistines said unto him, Make this fellow return, that he may go again to his place which thou hast appointed him, and let him not go down with us to battle, lest in the battle he be an adversary to us: for wherewith should he reconcile himself unto his master? should it not be with the heads of these men? Is not this David, of whom they sang one to another in dances, saying, Saul slew his thousands, and David his ten thousands? Then Achish called David, and said unto him, Surely, as the LORD *liveth, thou hast been upright, and thy going out and thy coming in with me in the host is good in my sight: for I have not found evil in thee since the day of thy coming unto me unto this day: nevertheless the lords favour thee not. Wherefore now return, and go in peace, that thou displease not the lords of the Philistines.* (I Samuel 29:1-7)

Didn't I warn you? David goes over to the enemy, proves his loyalty to the king of Goliath's home town, and is now ready to join the other Philistines in war against David's people. The man who refused to touch the insane King of Israel when he had a chance is now ready to do warfare against the people that he has been called to be King. Can it get any more bizarre? Remember in this chapter we're talking about being "sealed in providence." If God had allowed David to make this horrible mistake, Point B could certainly never happen. There is no way Israel would ever accept a king who had tried to kill them.

The above text illustrates both God's humor and His sovereignty. Sovereignty doesn't mean that God controls our decisions. But God is at work in all things for good for those who love Him (Romans 8:28 paraphrased). This means that God can untie the worst knot; He can redeem the worst mistakes as long as we don't abandon Him; He never forsakes us. David joins Achish as they meet the other Philistine kings to plan their attack on Israel. Suddenly some of the Philistine kings recognize David. Immediately, there is mumbling, "What's **he** doing here? That's David!" They must have thought that Achish had totally lost his mind. This is the guy who had killed tens of thousands of Philistines in battle. They had even made up songs about his battlefield exploits against their people. There is no way they are going to trust David, never! Achish assures them that he is truly a genuine traitor, but the other kings are not buying it for a minute.

David is sent away in disgrace. Now, where does he go? He's been rejected by the Philistines and he's a wanted man back in Israel. He has no nation, no people, and no purpose. We're not even close to the bottom, yet.

God will even take your failures and deep valley experiences and turn them for His glory and your good.

David has no choice but to return to Ziklag, the city given to him by Achish. When I read about his return to Ziklag I always think of the famous painting by James Earl Fraser titled, "The End of the Trail." You've probably seen it. It's one of the most truly pathetic paintings I've ever seen. It's a depiction of an Indian warrior on the back of a horse. The rider and horse alike are arched over in defeat and despair. You can feel the pathos of total defeat as you gaze at the masterpiece. That must have been what David looked like. He's completely defeated and humiliated. He can't even find a place with the enemy! His small band of followers accompany him as they limp back home. What are they going to tell their families? What of the future? Where will they turn?

Their despair turns to horror as they approach Ziklag. They see smoke rising on the horizon. As they approach the city, the unthinkable has happened. While they were away attempting to fight alongside the Philistines, another enemy, the Amalekites had attacked Ziklag, kidnapped their wives and children, and set the city on fire. All of their material possessions have gone up in smoke and their families taken by a vicious enemy. David and his men know exactly what is going to happen to their wives in the hands of the Amalekites. The journey to the depths of this valley is now complete. This is as low as it gets. God finally has David's full, undivided attention and it is here that David makes a choice that will determine whether he will ever get from his Point A to Point B.

And it came to pass, when David and his men were come to Ziklag on the third day, that the Amalekites had invaded the south, and Ziklag, and smitten Ziklag, and burned it with fire; and had taken the women captives, that were therein: they slew not any, either great or small, but carried them away, and went on their way. So David and his men came to the city, and, behold, it was burned with fire; and their wives, and their sons, and their daughters, were taken captives. Then David and the people that were with him lifted up their voice and wept, until they had no more power to weep. And David's two wives were taken captives, Ahinoam the Jezreelitess, and Abigail the wife of Nabal the Carmelite. And David was greatly distressed; for the people spake of stoning him, because the soul of all the people was grieved, every man for his sons and for his daughters: but David encouraged himself in the LORD *his God.* (1 Samuel 30:1-6)

Watch David's response and learn why God could take this miserable man to where He wanted him to be. Learn why he ultimately became a man after God's own heart. His first response is totally human. The text shows that he and his men weep until they have no more tears. Have you been there? I have. Our family went through our severe years of testing and dysfunction which we refer to as the "seven years of Hell." I remember walking the streets of our city all night long. I would leave the house around midnight and walk until sunrise. My heart would cry out to God, and I would weep until there were no more tears, then somehow tears would come again. It's very possible you've been there, too.

When you are there, don't waste your tears. Scripture declares that *joy comes in the morning.* Embrace that truth, stay the course—weep, cry out, refuse to run away or give us. Persist and persevere. Hang in there with God and you will come through the storm. Don't bail out; keep bailing. You cannot sink when God is with you.

David and his men weep but then David's men turn with anger against their leader. It was him that led them into battle with instead of against the enemy. Had they been home this wouldn't have happened! David's own men seriously discuss stoning him to death in retaliation for the loss of their families. The natural thing would be for David to run. He had done that before. He could run and hide from his men like he did from Saul. He was good at running. They would never find him. But something happens to David at the bottom of this dark valley. He stops depending on himself, his resources, his strength, and his cunning. In total "distress" David "encouraged himself in the Lord his God." Don't make the mistake that this means he took this lightly or flippantly. It was nothing of the sort. David is fully aware of his circumstances. He understands that there is no way out except for God's way. Before he had turned to his skills of avoidance, to his rag tag little army of men, and had even turned to his enemy. That has all failed. He has reached the end, the bottom, and he is now ready to surrender completely to God. He turns to the only real source of strength and wisdom—His God.

Much of this Point A to Point B journey is a heart thing.

Well, David was crowned King of Israel just like God said he would. He did reach Point B. Oh, his life was never easy and he certainly failed again and again. There was, of course, that whole Bathsheba thing, but David's heart was set to depend on God. That's what a "man after God's own heart" means. I thought for a long time that it meant that David's heart was just like God's. That notion is quickly destroyed if you simply read his life's story. There are multiple times that David is not anything like God even after he becomes king. But the fact remains that he was the greatest king in Israel's history because his heart was always pursuing after God. He often failed in this pursuit, but he never quit. When he sinned, he was devastated that he had failed in his pursuit of God's heart and he repents deeply. Read Psalm 51 sometime and witness a heart after God.

You see, much of this Point A to Point B journey is a heart thing. God is looking for hearts pursuing after Him. He desperately wants you to make it from Point A to Point B and He has a plan to accomplish it. I assure you the plan will not be the one you have chosen, but He does have a plan. He will accomplish it if you stay surrendered to Him. He will even take your failures and deep valley experiences and turn them for His glory and your good.

I said at the beginning of our study of David that he was unique from all other characters in scripture. If you take a quick look at the last words of the last book of the Bible, you will see something totally mind-blowing. There as Jesus gives His last words in the Book of books you will find this in Revelation 22:16, **"I am of the root and offspring of David."** Wow! With just a few words left in His Word, Jesus lays claim to the lineage of David. Oh, there was one more thing I almost forgot. Remember when we started looking at the life of David? We saw that David was chosen out of all the rest of Israel, hand- picked by the God of the Universe. Guess what? So were you! Ephesians 1:4 says, **"According as he hath chosen us in him before the foundation of the world, that we should be holy and without blame before him in love."** Out of the billions of people on this fallen planet, He chose you. You belong to Him. If He could do it with David, He can do it with you if your heart is pursuing Him. When you are in the depths of those lonely valleys, **remember Whose you are.**

Reflect and Apply

? *Are all the circumstances in your life telling you that you will never reach your Point B?*

? *Do you have some giants staring at you?*

? *Do you feel like God has abandoned you?*

? *Have you ever had something happen that caused you to weep until there were no more tears?*

? *Have you gotten to the place where you know there is no way out except for God's way?*

? *Do you understand that out of the billions of people on this fallen planet, He chose you?*

? *In the midst of your failures is your heart pursuing Him?*

Chapter Nine

BIBLICAL EXAMPLES OF GOD'S PROVIDENCE – ABRAHAM AND JOB

Abraham

J ust a reminder that what launched these character studies is Paul's admonition to a terribly backslidden church in Corinth. In spite of their "condition" he attempts to turn their attention to their "position" and assures them that in spite of their sin and rebellion, God was at work and was assuring them that "God is faithful" and preparing them for eternity. The faithfulness of God is displayed no better than in the story of the great patriarch Abraham. Abraham and Sarah were promised a baby by God Himself. The promise was Point A because this was not to be just any baby.

> *And, behold, the word of the LORD came unto him, saying, This shall not be thine heir; but he that shall come forth out of thine own bowels shall be thine heir. And he brought him forth abroad, and said, Look now toward heaven, and tell the stars, if thou be able to number them: and he said unto him, So shall thy seed be. And he believed in the LORD; and he counted it to him for righteousness.* (Genesis 15:4-6)

This promise would be repeated over and over to Abraham and his wife Sarah in different ways. Ultimately this "covenant" included the promise of a son who would be the father of a mighty nation that would one day inhabit all of the land of Canaan and that his "seed" would be the Messiah for all mankind. Wow! This is pretty heady stuff. A son, a people, a land, and most importantly, a Messiah is promised. Point A would be the reception of the promise and Point B would be the fulfillment of a son that would be the father of a mighty nation. At least that's the Point B in Abraham's lifetime. The ultimate fulfillment was the birth, life, death, and resurrection of Jesus.

Often there are a whole lot of "impossible" situations between Point A and Point B.

As we are seeing there is a whole lot that occurs between Point A and Point B and very little of it is what we expect or even want. That was certainly the case with Abraham. The promise is given and Abraham and Sarah wait and they wait. Then, they wait some more. They become impatient with God and the whole Ishmael debacle occurs. What a mess that was! More years pass and after twenty-five years when the promise becomes totally impossible due to their advanced age, God gives them their supernatural baby and they name him Isaac. I hope you're beginning to see that often there are a whole lot of "impossible" situations between Point A and Point B. That was certainly the case with Abe and Sarah. God intentionally stretched their faith to the point of breaking and then answered in such a manner that they couldn't take any credit. In case you haven't learned this yet, God does not take kindly to us taking the credit for things. His glory is of utmost importance to Him and it's not wise to take credit for what He alone can accomplish.

So, the promise is given, all kinds of things happen, years pass, and finally the baby arrives. End of story, right? We're safely at Point B, right? Wrong. This son has to live long enough to become the father of a mighty nation, remember? His birth is only the beginning of that part of the promise. Hang on; what follows is a wild ride.

Remember, this whole thing of God accomplishing His purpose in our lives is all about our heart.

I remember when our son came home from the hospital. Why was that so special? Well, it was the first time we saw him. He's adopted and he came to us straight from the hospital when he was four days old. We were excited beyond description. We had been praying for ten years for a baby. We had tried everything and decided that God wanted us to adopt. The day was here and yet we knew that with adoption there are many things that can go wrong at the last minute. We were staring out our front window at the driveway and suddenly we saw our attorney and his wife pull in. We could hardly contain ourselves. He was here! Our son! The one we had prayed for for such a long time. It's a day I will never forget and one of the happiest days of my life. My wife and I were finally parents of a beautiful baby boy! That must have been what it was like for Abraham and Sarah. They had waited for twenty-five years for this child. I can only imagine what a relationship Abraham had with his son. This was not just any child, he was a miracle in every way, and the future of the entire human race rested on the fulfillment of God's promise concerning this boy's lineage. I can't imagine a father and son being any tighter than Abraham and Isaac. Then came **that** day!

And it came to pass after these things, that God did tempt Abraham, and said unto him, Abraham: and he said, Behold, here I am. And he said, Take now thy son, thine only son Isaac, whom thou lovest, and get thee into the land of Moriah; and offer him there for a burnt offering upon one of the mountains which I will tell thee of. (Genesis 22:1-2)

What! Are you kidding me! Kill the promised son? The boy whose future will impact the entire human race? Are you serious? Oh yes, God was very serious and so was Abraham. Why would God do this and endanger the whole Point B for Abraham's life? Remember, this whole thing of God accomplishing His purpose in our lives is all about our heart. God is not very concerned about your physical stature, your talent or your natural abilities. He really isn't interested in who you are—but He wants to make sure that you never forget Whose You Are. He wants your heart—all of it. He refuses to take second place to any one, any idea, or any other pursuit in life except the pursuit of Him. In *The Pursuit of God*, A. W. Tozer comments, "God must do everything for us.

Our part is to yield and trust." That means total surrender. Remember, the hymn intones, "I surrender all," not, "I surrender some."

As a result, He will often test the attitudes and affections of our heart. That's the case here. This is a test of Abraham's heart. God has great things in store for Abraham and his son—but God must have Abraham's full attention and affection. Nothing and no one can be more important to Abraham than God Himself—so God puts Abraham to the ultimate test.

And Abraham rose up early in the morning, and saddled his ass, and took two of his young men with him, and Isaac his son, and clave the wood for the burnt offering, and rose up, and went unto the place of which God had told him. Then on the third day Abraham lifted up his eyes, and saw the place afar off. And Abraham said unto his young men, Abide ye here with the ass; and I and the lad will go yonder and worship, and come again to you. And Abraham took the wood of the burnt offering, and laid it upon Isaac his son; and he took the fire in his hand, and a knife; and they went both of them together. And Isaac spake unto Abraham his father, and said, My father: and he said, Here am I, my son. And he said, Behold the fire and the wood: but where is the lamb for a burnt offering? And Abraham said, My son, God will provide himself a lamb for a burnt offering: so they went both of them together. And they came to the place which God had told him of; and Abraham built an altar there, and laid the wood in order, and bound Isaac his son, and laid him on the altar upon the wood. And Abraham stretched forth his hand, and took the knife to slay his son. And the angel of the Lord *called unto him out of heaven, and said, Abraham, Abraham: and he said, Here am I. And he said, Lay not thine hand upon the lad, neither do thou any thing unto him: for now I know that thou fearest God, seeing thou hast not withheld thy son, thine only son from me. And Abraham lifted up his eyes, and looked, and behold behind him a ram caught in a thicket by his horns: and Abraham went and took the ram, and offered him up for a burnt offering in the stead of his son.* (Genesis 22:3-13)

I just can't imagine this scene. I really can't. I'm not sure I would have passed this test, but Abraham did. He absolutely knew that God would keep His promise about this son. He didn't know how. Maybe God would have to raise the boy from the dead, but he emphatically tells the servants that he **and** the boy would go, worship, and return. He knew the heart of God and God knew his heart.

Sometimes the journey from Point A to Point B, from your salvation to Christ-likeness takes turns that we would never dream of or choose. I would never have chosen for our family to go through the trials that we have. I was going to be a perfect father and raise perfect children. I had even read the Dobson books to assure it! I never dreamed of the heartache, sorrow, hurt, and failure that we experienced, but God was faithful even when I wasn't. When my wife and I had given up hope for our family and even each other, God was faithful.

That's what Paul was saying to the church at Corinth. That's what God demonstrated with the obedience of Abraham. God is faithful. Trust Him. Even when it looks impossible and when there is no hope, God is faithful. But God is also jealous. He wants all your heart, not part. He wanted all of Abraham's affection. I realize that this is an Old Testament story, but the principle has not changed. Jesus was the most loving, caring, compassionate individual who ever walked this earth, but He was also demanding. Listen to His words in Luke 14:26-27 and 33.

If any man come to me, and hate not his father, and mother, and wife, and children, and brethren, and sisters, yea, and his own life also, he cannot be my disciple. And whosoever doth not bear his cross, and come after me, cannot be my disciple. So likewise, whosoever he be of you that forsaketh not all that he hath, he cannot be my disciple.

Wow! That's pretty tough stuff. So, according to Jesus, if you're not willing to forsake anything and anyone you **cannot** be His disciple. That doesn't mean you neglect the people in your life or shirk your responsibilities with your family, your job or whatever. It's a matter of priorities. It's a matter of the heart. God wants to make you more like Christ. He wants to take you to your Point B and He has a plan to get you there, but your heart must be totally surrendered and you must be willing to trust God to take you on the path that He chooses. Is that really reasonable? Evidently, it is.

> *I beseech you therefore, brethren, by the mercies of God, that ye present your bodies a living sacrifice, holy, acceptable unto God, which is your reasonable service.* (Romans 12:1)

Now, what do we know about sacrifices in the Bible? We're not talking about missing your favorite TV show here to go to your kid's play at school. That may be a "sacrifice" in this culture, but it doesn't cut it on God's scale. A sacrifice was something that was totally consumed at the altar. A sacrifice had no rights. That's what Paul is talking about in Romans 12, a living sacrifice totally surrendered to God's plan and will. He says explicitly that this is "reasonable."

In Luke 14:27 Jesus says that it's necessary for a true disciple to "bear his cross." What does that mean? Well, certainly not what is often taught that "everyone has a cross to bear" implying that we all have difficulties and burdens that we have to carry through this life. A cross was not for bearing, it had one purpose—crucifixion. Crosses were only for dying. I would say that's pretty total surrender and that's exactly what Jesus demands of His disciples. It's not an option. If that's not your heart attitude, you may very well be a follower of Jesus but you're not a disciple if we are going to take the definition given by Jesus Himself.

You see, if you're born-again, you've been bought with a price. Paul gets to that principle over in Chapter 6 of I Corinthians. He tells the same people that he reminds of God's faithfulness in chapter one that they are "not their own" and have been "purchased" in chapter six. God is faithful and He is determined to work out His plan in your life, but you are a purchased possession. You've been purchased from the Devil himself with the precious blood of Jesus. You belong to Him and He has every right to your whole heart. You probably knew that, but occasionally we need to be reminded of **Whose we are.**

Job

There is an amazing ignorance of Scripture today. The statistics on biblical illiteracy are sobering. In the midst of all that Bible ignorance, there is character from God's Word that almost everyone is familiar with. Just mention the name Job and almost anyone will know that you're about to talk of suffering, trouble, struggle, and misery. His story is usually not known in detail, but the general theme is known by most. There are, however, some details of the story that most have missed.

Most trials are usually either for correction or perfection.

First is that Job's trial was not initiated by Satan, but by God Himself.

And the LORD said unto Satan, hast thou considered my servant Job, that there is none like him in the earth, a perfect and an upright man, one that feareth God, and escheweth evil?" (Job 1:8)

That word "escheweth" is significant here because it means "to perpetually turn away from." The implication is that the "turning away" is because of something harmful or wrong. Here is a man who perpetually turns away from anything evil and soon he will be the object of the very presence of evil. This testing is not something Job himself would have chosen.

Everyone knows that Satan brought a lot of really bad stuff into Job's life, but many are not aware that God started the whole thing by pointing out Job's goodness to the Devil. When we experience difficult periods in our life, it is natural to blame everything on the Devil but it is not always true. One of the earliest and most elementary lessons I learned from the pastor of my childhood is that most trials are usually either for correction or perfection. God is often attempting to bring sin to our attention to correct us as the writer of Hebrews states in Hebrews 12:6, "For whom the Lord loveth He chasteneth, and scourgeth every son whom He receiveth." This scourging and chastening are acts of love from a caring Father.

When God is perfecting us we can be absolutely assured that the fire prescribed will never be hotter than what is required or that we can endure.

The chastening is always in proportion to the amount of correction that is needed. The perfect father will never chasten more than is needed, but neither will he chasten less. When God is perfecting us we can be absolutely assured that the fire prescribed will never be hotter than what is required or that we can endure. I Corinthians 10:13 says, "Who will not suffer you to be tempted (tested) above what ye are able." Now, this is no big revelation, but when you are in the middle of that refining fire (Malachi 3:3; I Peter 1:7) it's difficult to believe or understand that God's hand is on the thermostat, but it's true.

When I was forced to take a sabbatical from the church that I had started I thought it was grossly unfair and unjust. How could I be removed from a ministry that I had given birth to? I had never experienced such humiliation and shame. I was convinced that this would destroy any future ministry, and with the resentment I felt for my wife I was also confident that my marriage had little hope. But God.... God knew I needed to be broken and He knew exactly where to "touch" me to bring about that brokenness. Ministry had become more important to me than anything or anyone. It had become far more about me than about Him. A precious pastor/mentor told me early in my ministry, "God will give you the power if you don't touch the glory." I certainly never experienced anything close to the trials of Job, but at the time I was certain that they were more than I could bear. The refining fire got extremely hot, but God clearly had His hand on the thermostat. It was exactly the purging, the cleansing, and the breaking that I needed. No more, no less. I have learned through experience that God will never test us more than is needed, but He will always do all that IS needed.

Whether we are in a period of correction or perfection, it's vital to understand that God is totally in control, and either way the circumstances surrounding us are for our ultimate good. Many people wear themselves out trying to figure out the "why" of the trial when all that is important is the "what." What is God teaching, what does God want to accomplish? If it is God who is teaching, then the important thing is to surrender to Him and trust that He will make His point clear in His time and in His way. He certainly did with Job.

When you are in the middle of that refining fire it's difficult to believe or understand that God's hand is on the thermostat, but it's true.

While many wear themselves out trying to figure out the why instead of the what, others beat themselves up assuming that God is angry with them and is "punishing" them for something they've done. In forty plus years of ministry I've heard countless people ask me why God is punishing them. My answer often shocks the bewildered Christian. If you are born-again, then God cannot punish you. The truth is God cannot and will not punish any of His children. How is that possible? When Jesus hung on the cross of Calvary, He received all of God's punishment for all of sin for all of time.

Scripture is clear that God is "angry at sin" (Romans 1:18). His character demands that He judge sin; it's His nature. It is tragic that many teachers today deny this important biblical truth and present only half of God's character. Denying or hiding God's righteous anger emasculates God and robs people of who God really is. What's the big deal about God's mercy if it's not really needed? If God is only love then what's the big whoop about grace? It is absolutely true that God must punish sin, but for the believer in Christ all of that punishment was poured out upon Jesus. He took their place and paid the full price for their salvation. Because of that, God cannot punish His children as Jesus already took it all upon Himself. It is absolutely wrong for the Christian to assume that they are being punished by God. What about those who are not born-again believers? Sadly, if they have not trusted Christ to be their substitute, then they will pay for their own sin throughout eternity. It's either "Jesus paid it all" or you will pay it all.

It is absolutely true that God must punish sin, but for the believer in Christ all of that punishment was poured out upon Jesus.

What's the big difference between punishment and chastisement? Is it really that big a deal if you're in the middle of it? The answer is yes, it's a huge deal. Punishment says, "You did it, now you're going to pay for it." Punishment cares little about your response. You do the crime, you do the time. It's totally punitive and without compassion. Chastisement, on the other hand, is all about love. Chastisement is always for the good of the one on the end of the chastisement. Chastisement seeks to correct, to help, to strengthen, and to shape. When I was a kid and I was at the other end of my Dad's "instrument of chastisement," I really didn't care whether it was chastisement or punishment. All I knew was it hurt and it was tough to sit down. When we are the subject of God's loving chastisement, it is often just as difficult to thank Him for His "loving" rod of correction but it is a mark of maturity.

Therefore, the second thing that is often misunderstood about Job's trial is that it was all for his benefit and good. "What!" you say. "He lost everything—his kids, the love of his wife, his house, his herds, his possessions, and his health! Sounds like it was really good for him!" You're probably wondering what happened to all the Point A and Point B stuff in this portion of the book. Let's address both; why this was "good" and the Point A and Point B of this story.

Point A would be God's recognition of Job's faith and faithfulness. There was "none like him in the earth" according to God. At that point Satan accused Job of serving God only because God had blessed him and protected him. In response, God told Satan to have at it with certain restrictions and assured Satan that even after severe testing Job would remain faithful. That would bring Job to Point B which is the perfection brought about by Satan's attacks. Note that this does not contradict what we've just discussed about most correcting and perfecting comes from God. Job is clearly attacked by Satan, but God is never out of control and puts clear limits on what Satan can do. Whatever Satan does to you, it is never out of God's sovereign hand.

The overwhelming lesson that we must learn from the life of Job is that sometimes there is a tremendous amount of pain and suffering between Point A and Point B, but at no point was Job abandoned by God. At no point was Job's suffering more than he could bear. At no point was Job hidden from God's providential hand. The fire of testing was severe, far more severe than anything I've ever endured and hopefully more than you will ever endure, but God had His hand firmly on the thermostat. Even Satan himself could not go beyond God's sovereign limits.

So, our family experienced those "seven years of Hell." It was a time of testing and trial that at times I was convinced was beyond my limits of endurance. From a purely human standpoint, it probably was. But God knew what He was doing. My failure as a husband, father, and pastor was thrown in my face by the evil enemy of my soul. He almost convinced me that life had spun totally out of control and there was no hope. No, I never thought of taking my life, but I pleaded that God would. I was at the very bottom, the bitter end, and exactly where God wanted me to be. The only place where I could learn the lessons that God knew I needed. Painful? Indescribable. Feeling abandoned? Oh yes. Without hope? Close. Forgotten? Absolutely not.

So does Job make it to Point B? In spite of horrible trials, miserable friends, and bitter doubts—yes. When you come to the end of this incredible story you find this amazing testimony of Job's latter years.

So the LORD blessed the latter end of Job more than his beginning: for he had fourteen thousand sheep, and six thousand camels, and a thousand yoke of oxen, and a thousand she asses. He had also seven sons and three daughters. (Job 42:12-13)

Now, if you compare that with the first chapter when we are introduced to Job, that's exactly twice what he had before the attacks of Satan (Job 1:1-3). I can hear some shouting, "But wait! He lost seven sons and three daughters and at the end he only had seven sons and three daughters." You would be right if we didn't believe the Word of God. I am convinced that all of those sons and daughters that were "lost" during his Satanic trial were waiting for Job when he died and when you get to Heaven yourself you'll find that Job has fourteen sons and six daughters with him.

God brought Job to a wonderful Point B in spite of the extraordinary suffering, anguish, loss, and trials in between. He was firmly held in God's sovereign hand because He was God's possession. God takes care of His kids. When we cannot see His hand we can trust His heart.

When you are facing Job-like trials and even when you find yourself under the direct attack of the Enemy, **remember Whose you are!**

Reflect and Apply

? *Do you agree that there are a whole lot of "impossible" situations between Point A and Point B?*

? *Have you experienced this in your own life?*

? *Has God been intentionally stretching your faith to the point of breaking?*

? *Have you learned God does not take kindly to us taking the credit for what He alone can accomplish?*

? *Are you at a place where you are willing to forsake anything and anyone to be His disciple?*

? *Does that mean you neglect the people in your life or shirk your responsibilities with your family, your job or whatever?*

? *Are you at a place where you are willing to trust God to take you on the path that He chooses?*

? *What is God teaching you and what does God want to accomplish in the midst of the trial you are in right now?*

? *Have you been in the habit of blaming everything on the Devil?*

? *Has the story of Job changed your opinion in this area?*

? *Have you been assuming you are being punished by God?*

? *Are you a child of God? Why does that make a difference?*

Chapter Ten

BIBLICAL EXAMPLES OF GOD'S PROVIDENCE – PAUL AND THE NEW TESTAMENT CHURCH

Paul

Time, paper, and ink simply does not afford a detailed look at all the illustrations of God's providential hand at work in the lives of those who belong to Him, but it's prudent to look to at least a few illustrations from the New Testament as well as those we've examined from the Old Testament. The sovereign hand of God is just as active in the New Testament as it was in the Old. God continues to bring those that are His from Point A to Point B simply because they **are** His and they **are** sealed in His providence as Paul reminded the saints in Corinth. In fact, Paul could remind the Corinthian saints of this wonderful principle because he had experienced it himself on many occasions. One of the more obscure, yet powerful, instances of God's providential hand in the life of Paul is found in Romans 15:24-29.

Whensoever I take my journey into Spain, I will come to you: for I trust to see you in my journey, and to be brought on my way thitherward by you, if first I be somewhat filled with your company. But now I go unto Jerusalem to minister unto the saints. For it hath pleased them of Macedonia and Achaia to make a certain contribution for the poor saints which are at Jerusalem. It hath pleased them verily; and their debtors they are. For if the Gentiles have been made partakers of their spiritual things, their duty is also to minister unto them in carnal things. When therefore I have performed this, and have sealed to them this fruit, I will come by you into Spain. And I am sure that, when I come unto you, I shall come in the fullness of the blessing of the gospel of Christ.

Paul is wrapping up this epistle to the Christians at Rome, and he wants them to know what his plans are. He desperately wants to see them in person but he has a few things that he needs to take care of first. He has a desire to take a quick trip to Spain. We're not quite sure what the purpose of that trip was to be and history does not record that he ever made it. What we do know is that he is certain he will be seeing the Roman Christians in person after he makes a quick trip to Jerusalem. We know from 1 Corinthians 16:1-4 and 2 Corinthians 9:1-15 that the purpose of the trip to Jerusalem was to deliver financial help to the poor saints in the Jerusalem church. He had received this money from Gentiles who had sacrificially given to help their Jewish brethren. Paul was hopeful that this generosity would help erase some of the suspicion that a few of the Jewish Christians in Jerusalem had towards their Gentile brethren.

If you were to translate Romans 15:24-29 into contemporary language, Paul would be saying to the Roman Christians, "Hey guys, I'm really looking forward to seeing you all. I think I'll head over to see you right after my quickie trip to Spain, but first I've got to head down to Jerusalem and drop off a really cool offering that the Gentile brothers gave. Some in the Jerusalem fellowship have had it really tough and this offering is going to blow them away. When I get finished in Jerusalem, I'll pop by Spain and head your way. When I get there we're going to have a great time and I'll tell you all about the trip!" He seems to indicate that the whole trip is going to be a piece of cake, and when he makes it to Rome they'll have a great time together. This was not the case at all.

Paul was confident that God wanted him to go to Rome. He had no idea that this would be his final Point B and that he would end up dying there, but he knew God wanted him to make the trip. We also know that he made it, but there was a whole lot that he did not plan on between Point A and Point B.

The story is very familiar so we won't go great detail. If you want to study the entire story you simply need to read Acts 21-28. Paul takes his trip to Jerusalem and does indeed deliver the offering to the poor saints in the church, but that's where the expected ended. Paul decides to do a little preaching while he's in the City of David and his preaching causes a riot. He is dragged out of the Temple and almost killed by an angry mob. At the last minute he is rescued by Roman centurions. Although saved from death by the Roman soldiers, they immediately arrest him and put him in chains (Acts 21:27-33). The poor Roman soldiers have no idea what to do with him and it's not long before Paul convinces them to let him preach again to the same mob that almost killed him! You have to love Paul's determination! From there Paul is bounced back and forth between the Jewish leaders who wanted Paul dead and the Roman leaders who had no idea what to do with this wild man!

Paul finally plays the citizenship card and declares that he is a Roman citizen and appeals his case to Caesar. The Jews are furious, the Romans are perplexed, and Paul is in for a wild, wild ride. After a long delay Paul is loaded on to a boat headed for Rome. So Paul gets a free, all expense-paid trip to Point B, right? The ship was not exactly a non-stop luxury liner to Rome. Paul is bounced from ship to ship and port to port. Subsequently his ship encounters the storm of the century with its own special name, Euroclydon. The ship almost sinks, the crew has to throw all the cargo overboard to no avail, and the ship finally crashes and sinks. Miraculously everyone on board survives and they are shipwrecked on the island of Malta.

All the drama is gone, right? Paul is bitten by a venomous snake, but God is not finished with him yet and he certainly has not reached his Point B so even a poisonous snake cannot thwart God's plan for Paul's life. Paul may have been the great apostle that wrote nearly three quarters of the New Testament, but that's not what preserved him and protected him. Who Paul was was not nearly as important as whose Paul was. He was purchased by the precious blood of Jesus and nothing and no one could stand in the way of what God wanted to do through His purchased possession. Paul's job was not to figure out all of God's plans but to simply surrender to it. His WILL for us is to be saved, healed, and delivered through His Son Jesus Christ. In reality the will of God is the same for every believer. Within that will are His plans. Those plans are unique for every Christian.

Consider these promises
Jeremiah 29:11-12 declares, "For I know the *thoughts* that I think toward you, saith the LORD, *thoughts* of peace, and not of evil, to give you an expected end."

Psalm 33:11-12 assures, "The counsel of the LORD standeth forever, the *thoughts* of his heart to all generations."

The Hebrew word for *thoughts* may also be translated *plans*. So, when God's will and thoughts for you births plans (notice it's plural not singular) in you, His grace is so prodigious that if you fail to accomplish the first plan, He'll give you another. Remember that Thomas Edison had thousands of filaments he tested for a light bulb and failed thousands of times. But he did give up. The same is true for you. God gives us a multitude of *plans* because He knows that we can mess up even the most perfect plan from Him. Just remember, that when God has birthed a plan, we can't fail if we don't give up. Never give up on what God has promised you. So, don't forget that God has wonderful and good plans for your life and He will accomplish them as long as you surrender to His sovereignty. You are sealed in His providence, just like Paul.

Who Paul was, was not nearly as important as whose Paul was.

Paul does finally arrive in Rome and God gives him an incredible ministry there, but from a jail cell! That was certainly not anything like Paul had planned. God's plan was far greater than Paul's plan, and we know from Philippians 4:22 that Paul even led many of Caesar's household to Christ! God's plan is always better and more fruitful than ours.

Between Paul's promise in Romans 15 to come and visit the saints in Rome (Point A) and Paul's ultimate arrival (Point B) there are riots, mobs, beatings, arrests, conspiracies, chains, storms, ship-wrecks, poisonous snakes, and jail cells, but God was never out of control. I don't know what you might be experiencing right now in your life. I have no idea what storms you might be facing in your life, your marriage, your job, your health—but I know God has a plan. You may not be able to see it and if you did you might not understand it, but if you will daily surrender to His plan God will never forsake you. If you have trusted Christ you are God's purchased possession and you are just as important to Him as Paul was. **Remember Whose You Are!**

God's plan is always better and more fruitful than ours.

The New Testament Church

Until now we've focused on the providential hand of God on individuals, but let's not forget that this entire study was prompted by Paul's letter to a church, a body of believers. His words were certainly applicable to individuals, but he wrote it to the church at Corinth. God obviously cares about individuals, but He also has enormous care for His church. After all, Jesus died for His Bride—the Church.

There is no doubt that the Church is under attack today and many churches have succumbed to the attack and abandoned truth. The mainline denominational churches, for the most part, long ago departed from the faith and have become social clubs rather than the citadels of truth that God intended for them to be. Compromise and capitulation to a secular world-view has resulted in steep decline and for some total death. Most denominational churches have faced a continual decline every year for over forty years. As a result, the Christian Church in America continues to have less and less influence on culture, government, and society in general. Today, the world has had much more influence on the church than vice-versa. This is not God's plan.

The Church was to be a "light" in the midst of darkness, and an oasis of truth in a desert of error. At the same time, many churches that have held the line theologically have become so much like the world to "reach" the world that they also have lost much of their transformative influence in their communities. The church has often been likened to a "ship" that is a float in a vast ocean called the world. We have often heard of the "Old Ship of Zion" or "The Gospel Ship" and a myriad of other nautical references to the church. If we take that allegory and examine it we quickly realize that it is completely normal for a ship to be surrounded by water. That's a good thing. However, when the water begins to flood the ship, that's a problem. It's clear that in many areas the church has sprung a leak. Does this destroy God's ultimate plan? Absolutely not.

Christ died for His church and He will continue to work wherever He finds people who love Him and are seeking His heart. I still believe that God can bring revival. Will we ever see a great national revival in America? Only God knows that but my heart desires that God's people in local churches like yours will seek Him with all their heart and pray for revival in your part of the world.

God loves to restore, revive, and renew His people.

Granted, there is much to be discouraged about when you look at the condition of the American Church, but God always has a remnant and He has promised that even the "gates of Hell" will not prevail against the Bride of Christ (Matthew 16:18). The church today is obviously as sick as the church at Corinth was, but there is always hope and God will maintain a Gospel witness anywhere He finds His people who are willing to surrender to the authority of His Word. The church at Corinth was in spiritual ICU but they were still willing to respond to Paul's reminders and rebuke. God loves to restore, revive, and renew His people. The church is His church, His body, His people, and His Bride and He will respond to those who remember **Whose** they are.

This principle is illustrated in a magnificent manner in Acts chapter 12 where we read that the Church at Jerusalem was under fierce attack. They were under fire from the Roman government because the Romans were frightened that the followers of "the King of the Jews" would organize a revolt against the empire. They needed to be eliminated. They were also under attack from the Jewish religion. The Jews had turned Jesus over to the Romans as a "blasphemer" and subversive and demanded that He be crucified. The death of Jesus only raised the level of anger and resentment toward His followers. They were determined to destroy this threat to their religious way of life.

In Acts 8 you learn that because of this severe persecution most of the membership in the church had fled for their lives and were "scattered abroad" leaving a small remnant behind under the leadership of Peter. In essence, the church at Jerusalem was under attack by the most powerful political force on the earth—Rome, and the most powerful religious force in the region—the Jews. Not a very rosy picture!

Now about that time Herod the king stretched forth his hands to vex certain of the church. And he killed James the brother of John with the sword. And because he saw it pleased the Jews, he proceeded further to take Peter also. (Then were the days of unleavened bread.) And when he had apprehended him, he put him in prison, and delivered him to four quaternions of soldiers to keep him; intending after Easter to bring him forth to the people. (Acts 12:1-4)

Talk about a bad situation! The primary leader of the church at Jerusalem is sitting in prison, guarded by sixteen big burly Roman soldiers, waiting to be executed. It's obvious that Herod, with the assistance of the Jews, will come after the rest of the remnant after Peter has his head chopped off. Things are not looking good at all for Christ's church. In fact, it is hard to imagine things being even worse; until they actually get worse!

And when Herod would have brought him forth, the same night Peter was sleeping between two soldiers, bound with two chains: and the keepers before the door kept the prison. And, behold, the angel of the Lord came upon him, and a light shined in the prison: and he smote Peter on the side, and raised him up, saying, Arise up quickly. And his chains fell off from his hands. And the angel said unto him, Gird thyself, and bind on thy sandals. And so he did. And he saith unto him, Cast thy garment about thee, and follow me. And he went out, and followed him; and wist not that it was true which was done by the angel; but thought he saw a vision. (Acts 12:6-9)

You might be saying, "Wait, you said things got worse. Peter was just delivered miraculously from certain death. That's awesome!" Well, it was a wonderful thing, but do you really think that Herod was going to just give up and stop persecuting the church? Seriously? I can only imagine his rage when he discovered that his prize prisoner had escaped and no one knew how, where or why. In fact, Acts 12:20 reveals that

Herod was enraged and immediately executed all the guards who were seemingly responsible for Peter's escape. He's really ticked and common sense would tell you that he was now thoroughly determined to find the followers of Christ and take care of them all. Now, it really is hard to imagine how things could be more bleak for this infant church. Could things possibly get worse? Well, as a matter of fact, yes.

And upon a set day Herod, arrayed in royal apparel, sat upon his throne, and made an oration unto them. And the people gave a shout, saying, It is the voice of a god, and not of a man. (Acts 12:21-22)

The Jewish historian Josephus describes in detail the "royal" robes of Herod. They were actually woven with genuine gold and silver thread. In the sun, they would have been blinding as they reflected the sun. It must have been garments like this that Herod wore on this day. His oration was mesmerizing and the people of Jerusalem proclaimed him to be a god and not a man. His power and authority had reached its zenith. How easy it would have been for him to unleash his anger and vengeance against these seemingly helpless Christians to atone for his utter humiliation in the case of Peter's escape. Now, things really did look bad for the church, really bad. Their future was seriously in doubt as the two most powerful human forces of the region were united against the church.

In the light of these horrible circumstances it would be very easy to forget about God's providence. Does Herod wipe out the church, the church die, and the gospel stopped?

And immediately the angel of the Lord smote him, because he gave not God the glory: and he was eaten of worms, and gave up the ghost. (Acts 12:23)

Herod died a horrible and humiliating death. God took care of the church's greatest threat in just one, short verse of scripture—an asterisk on the page of history, just a brief moment in time. Your problems, your enemies or the problems and enemies of His church are never a big deal for God. They only seem big to us. God is never worried, never frets, and is absolutely never, ever out of control.

But the word of God grew and multiplied. (Acts 12:24)

Look at what God did in two short verses! In verse 22 all is lost, things look terrible, the church was dead, and God's people are defeated. There seemed to be no way out! Two verses later the greatest enemy of the church was dead and the Word of God was growing and multiplying. I'm certain the folks in that Jerusalem church were totally shocked, but God wasn't. He knew all along what He would do and how to fulfill His plan. Even the entire Roman Empire was no big obstacle to God.

But wait! What about all that Point A to Point B stuff! What does this whole Acts 12 story have to do with that? Point A for the church is in Matthew 28:19-20.

> *Go ye therefore, and teach all nations, baptizing them in the name of the Father, and of the Son, and of the Holy Ghost: Teaching them to observe all things whatsoever I have commanded you: and, lo, I am with you always, even unto the end of the world. Amen.*

These are the last words Jesus gave to His disciples. They are His final instructions and reveal God's plan for His Church. They were to go into the entire world, proclaim the Gospel and make disciples. The development and implementation of a comprehensive movement of world evangelism and discipleship would be Point B. Things got off to an incredible start. The first move towards Point B was obviously the day of Pentecost. What a day! Three thousand men were saved and added to the church. We have no idea how many women and children would have been included. The church literally exploded in growth. Shortly after the day of Pentecost another 5,000 came to Christ. Wow, getting to Point B would be a walk in the park!

In Acts 8 things seem to start falling apart. Enormous persecution arose against the church and the overwhelming majority of the church members had to flee the city for their lives. Was God's plan thwarted? As they were dispersed, Acts 8:4 says, "Therefore they that were scattered abroad went everywhere preaching the word." They dispersed throughout the world taking the gospel with them. That sounds a whole lot like the purpose of the Great Commission.

Then we come to the text that we have been looking at in Acts 12. All is bleak, all is lost, all is gloomy, and things go from bad to worse and then even more worse. All seems lost and God's plan seems to be destroyed. God displays His providential hand and the Word multiples and the church is preserved. It gets better, so much better! If you're a student of church history, what happens immediately after this episode in Jerusalem is recorded in Acts 13:1-3.

> *Now there were in the church that was at Antioch certain prophets and teachers; as Barnabas, and Simeon that was called Niger, and Lucius of Cyrene, and Manaen, which had been brought up with Herod the tetrarch, and Saul. As they ministered to the Lord, and fasted, the Holy Ghost said, Separate me Barnabas and Saul for the work whereunto I have called them. And when they had fasted and prayed, and laid their hands on them, they sent them away.*

The modern mission movement is given birth in Acts 13:1-3, a movement that continues today over 2,000 years later! As a result, multiplied millions of people have trusted Christ, been baptized, and have become disciples. To look chronologically at scripture, in six short verses (Acts 12:22-13:2) you go from what seems to be the total destruction of God's plan to what is the beginning of its ultimate fulfillment. Only God can do that. At times things looked bleak, even impossible. There was an enormous amount of circumstances between Point A and Point B, but God was always in control. You see, the church belongs to God. The church is His bride and He purchased her with His blood. He will take care of those who are His. If you are bought with His blood, if you have trusted Christ as your Savior, then, please remember **Whose** you are.

I have no idea where or what your Point A was and I know even less about your Point B, but God knows it all and has a plan. Often you will not see His plan nor understand it. That's not your responsibility. God never told us to "figure it out." He simply wants us to trust Him. That's our responsibility. Surrender includes our trusting and obeying God. God will take care of everything if we are willing to surrender (completely in trust and obedience). We surrender all to His sovereign hand and His providential plan. Are you willing to trust Him today and place your life in His hands?

I love a story I once heard on the topic of surrender and revival. The great revivalist of the past, Gipsy Smith was in the middle of a wonderful outpouring of the spirit of God in a local church. The meeting that was scheduled for two weeks continued week after week as God brought people to repentance and revival. A pastor in a city many miles away heard about the revival and felt compelled to visit the revival and see for himself what God was doing. He was amazed at what he saw and experienced. He felt an overwhelming desire deep within his breast for such a moving of God's Spirit to visit his congregation. At the close of the evening meeting the pastor waited to speak to the renowned preacher. He asked Preacher Smith how he could have this kind of revival at his church. What was the secret to revival? Gipsy Smith turned to the pastor and told him to go home and lock himself in his bedroom. When the door was locked, get on his knees on the floor and draw a circle around himself. Then Smith told him to begin praying that God would bring revival to the inside of that circle and determine that he would not leave the room until revival had truly come. Revival does not begin with "them" it begins with me. Each day, begin your day by surrendering everything—yes, everything inside your own circle. Then let God take care of the details outside the circle. After all, He owns all that is within that circle anyway and is in control of all that is without.

> *What? Know ye not that your body is the temple of the Holy Ghost which is in you, which ye have of God, and ye are not your own? For ye are bought with a price: therefore glorify God in your body, and in your spirit, which are God's.* (1 Corinthians 6:19-20)

My friend, my dear reader—can I ask you a very personal question? Right now what does your surrender look like? Are you willing to put it all in His hands? Will you trust Him for all that is between A and B in your life?

I want to encourage you right now as you are reading this. Whatever you are struggling with or going through isn't a surprise to God. His plans and thoughts for you are good. He not only knows your past and present, your future is in His hands. Trust Him. As a born-again believer, you no longer belong to yourself. "Ye belong to Christ" declares Mark 9:41). You are His and He is yours. He will take care of His own. Whatever is happening in your life right now is part of God's plan to take you to your Point B—the likeness of Christ. When you have doubts, when you struggle, when you try to do things in your own strength, when you resist God's hand, when you try to run from His plan, **Remember Whose You Are!**

Reflect and Apply

? *Are you willing to trust Him today and place your life in His hands?*

? *Do you understand that who you are is not nearly as important as Whose you are?*

? *Whose are you?*

? *Right now, what are you planning on doing to surrender to God's plan for your life?*

Final Word

WALK IN THE KNOWLEDGE OF *WHOSE YOU ARE!*

I n the very beginning of this book, I pointed out the deplorable spiritual condition of the church at Corinth. They were immature, divided, carnal, rebellious, and contentious. What struck me and what challenged me to write this book was the manner in which Paul addressed these miserable Christians. I was shocked that he didn't begin by confronting them with their sin. Granted, he does that later in his epistle and he's actually pretty tough on them, but he begins with encouragement, not condemnation. He begins, not by bringing to their attention their failures, but by reminding them of their relationship with Christ. He reminds them that they are

1) Sanctified in Position,
2) Saintly in Purpose,
3) Sufficient in Power, and
4) Sealed in Providence.

How did that strategy work? They were clearly in a total mess when he writes his first letter. How did they respond? Well, I'll let Paul tell you because he wrote them another letter. We're not sure how much time has passed between I Corinthians and II Corinthians but it was certainly long enough for God to do a powerful work in their body. Here is part of what Paul tells them in the second letter.

For though I made you sorry with a letter, I do not repent, though I did repent: for I perceive that the same epistle hath made you sorry, though it were but for a season. Now I rejoice, not that ye were made sorry, but that ye sorrowed to repentance: for ye were made sorry after a godly manner, that ye might receive damage by us in nothing. For godly sorrow worketh repentance to salvation not to be repented of: but the sorrow of the world worketh death. For behold this selfsame thing, that ye sorrowed after a godly sort, what carefulness it wrought in you, yea, what clearing of yourselves, yea, what indignation, yea, what fear, yea, what vehement desire, yea, what zeal, yea, what revenge! In all things ye have approved yourselves to be clear in this matter. (2 Corinthians 7:8-11)

I absolutely love that last part: "In all things ye have approved yourselves to be clear in this matter." Isn't that awesome! This sad, pathetic church was convicted by God's Spirit, repented of their sin, and experienced a genuine revival. It all began with a reminder of their position in Christ. They were reminded that they had been made saints by the power of regeneration. They had been given everything they needed to live a victorious life, and they were reminded that God was faithful and had a perfect plan for their lives. Those truths and Paul's subsequent confrontation concerning their actual sins brought about a deep work of revival. The work of God in our lives is a wonderful, supernatural work but as we have seen it is not always pleasant. When I began writing this book I had completely lost my voice due to paralyzed vocal chords and I was uncertain whether I would ever be able to speak again. I am extremely grateful to report that the paralysis is completely gone and my voice is totally normal again. It was a painful and frightening Point A to Point B, but God is faithful and I am continually reminded of **Whose** I am.

God's work in us may be painful, unpleasant, difficult, and challenging. Still, it is necessary. I love the plenteous ways that God reminds us that He is in control. Recently I came across a beautiful poem that Joni Tada, founder of Joni & Friends, wrote in my wife's Bible many years ago. Joni—a quadriplegic—wrote this with a pen in her mouth. The author is unknown:

When God wants to drill a man,
And thrill a man,
And skill a man
When God wants to mold a man
To play the noblest part;

When He yearns with all His heart
To create so great and bold a man
That all the world shall be amazed,
Watch His methods, watch His ways!

How He ruthlessly perfects
Whom He royally elects!
How He hammers him and hurts him,
And with mighty blows converts him

Into trial shapes of clay which
Only God understands;
While his tortured heart is crying
And he lifts beseeching hands!

How He bends but never breaks
When his good He undertakes;
How He uses whom He chooses,
And which every purpose fuses him;
By every act induces him
To try His splendor out-
God knows what He's about.

I'm wondering today as you read these words where you are in your spiritual life. What is it that you need to be reminded of? Have you been overwhelmed so much by your condition that you have forgotten your position? Have you slipped into despair and defeat? Start today to meditate on **who** you are and **Whose** you are. Ask God to reveal to you your rebellious flesh so that He has permission to bring it to your attention and then immediately surrender it at the foot of the cross. I am praying that as you read these words that if it is comfort that you need, God will provide it to you by reminding you of **who you are.**

You are:
- **His precious child,**
- **His redeemed one,**
- **His loved one,**
- **His forgiven one,**
- **His accepted one.**

If it is conviction that you need, I am praying that He will remind you of **Whose you are. You are** a purchased possession, purchased by the Blood of Christ. You are not your own.

You may feel depressed, abandoned, orphaned, rejected, and alone.
Remember Whose you are.

You may think your situation is hopeless, impossible, or overwhelming.
Remember Whose you are.

You may be experiencing illness, pain, suffering, or anguish.
Remember Whose you are.

You may be tempted to quit, sin, fail, run away, or end it all.
Remember Whose you are.

You may feel that your circumstances are spiraling completely out of control.
Remember Whose you are.

You may feel that the Devil is trying to destroy you and those you love.
Remember Whose you are.

God takes good care of His possessions! Never forget that no matter what is happening and how you feel—God is in control and He might simply be waiting for your total surrender. I urge you to reach out to a Christian friend, pastor, counselor, or church. Someone who belongs to Christ will listen, help, pray, and walk with you because of *Whose you are. Go back often to chapter two and start meditating on the "In Christ" verses. Don't just read them, meditate on them. Look seriously at your position in Christ and see if your present* **condition** *(how you feel about yourself) stacks up to your* **position** *(What God says about you)—then decide who you are going to believe—your flesh or God. Never forget Whose you are.*

Would you allow me to pray for you?

Dear Father, because I believe in your providential hand—I am absolutely confident that the person who just finished this simple book did not do so by accident. I am also completely certain that you are right now, at this very minute, working out your plan in their life. They may not realize it, see it or understand it but I believe that you are at work in every circumstance surrounding them. If they have been born again—Open their eyes, Father, to see the truth of their position in Christ and open their heart to respond, in surrender, to the plan that you have chosen to conform them to the image of Christ. If they have never trusted your son, Jesus, as their Savior—I pray that at this very moment they would confess their sin and accept the gift of salvation made possible through the sacrifice of Jesus on the Cross. Finish the work that you have begun through the power of your Spirit and the ministry of your Word. May this very moment be the time when this precious individual understands Whose they are. Wherever they are at this moment, may it become an altar where they offer themselves completely and wholly to you.

I pray this in the precious and wonderful name that is above all names—the name of Jesus.

Amen.

ABOUT THE AUTHOR

B ob Burney was born and raised in Southern California but now resides with his wife, Joy in Columbus, Ohio. Bob is the proud father of three and grandfather of eight.

He and his wife, Joy, founded Calvary Bible Baptist Church in the Columbus area where he served as senior pastor for 25 years. In 2001, he resigned the pastorate to found CrossPower Ministries with his wife. Together they travel the United States doing Marriage Conferences, Revivals, Family Conferences and what they love best – CrossPower Weekends–where Christians are taught how to appropriate their incredible riches in Christ.

Bob has ministered in over 20 countries of the world and is a popular conference speaker. He has served on the Ohio Governor's Commission of Faith Based and Community Initiative under three different administrations. In his radio work, Bob's program – Bob Burney Live! - was nominated for the National Talk Show of the year by the National Association of Religious Broadcasters and was awarded Talk Show Host of the Year by Salem Media.

To order a copy of this book go to www.rememberwhoseyouare.com or call 614 890-1974.

To book Bob and Joy Burney for a meeting in your local church go to www.crosspower.net or call 614 890-1974.

CPSIA information can be obtained at www.ICGtesting.com
Printed in the USA
BVOW01s1211060414

349682BV00001B/3/P